SKIING REAL SNOW

Skiing Real Snow

THE HANDBOOK OF OFF-PISTE SKIING

Martyn Hurn

The Crowood Press

First published in 1987 by
The Crowood Press
Ramsbury, Marlborough
Wiltshire SN8 2HE

British Library Cataloguing in Publication Data

Hurn, Martyn
    Skiing real snow: the handbook of off-piste skiing.
    1. Skis and skiing
    I. Title
    796.93   GV854
ISBN 1 85223 021 5

Dedicated to all those with whom I have adventured.

Picture Credits

Front of jacket: Terry Storry
Back of jacket: All-Sport Photographic Ltd
All-Sport Photographic Ltd: Figs 77, 78, 79, 80, 81, 82
Europa Sport Collection: Figs 5, 39, 41, 43, 75
Peter Finklair: Fig 6
Tim Hawkins: Figs 16, 23, 37, 38, 92, 100–106, 116–122,
    132–138, 142, 143
George Reed: Fig 156
John Shedden: Figs 1, 42, 68, 70
Terry Storry: Fig 65
The remainder are by the author

Typeset by Alacrity Phototypesetters,
Banwell Castle, Weston-super-Mare
Printed in Spain by Graficromo s.a., Cordoba

Contents

Acknowledgements

In any book of this nature the author only really acts as an editor, a collector of ideas that have come from a multitude of sources, not least of which are the many pupils and fellow instructors that I have had the very real pleasure of being able to share my mountain days with.

Special thanks, however, must go to Wendy and Alan Hughes for the long hours they spent with me discussing various ideas; to John Shedden, and the staff of Plas-Y-Brenin for their valuable criticisms of the text; to my friends Adrian and John who helped so much in the later stages; to Tim Hawkins for his work on the photography and to Europa Sport and Mike Browne of Snow and Rock who supplied the equipment for the photographs; to Steve Booth and Denise Long for their perseverance with the diagrams; and finally to Nance who gave me the initial impetus to undertake the project.

Fig 1 Good dynamic skiing.

Preface

I was skiing in the high Himalayas. The resort consisted of one thirty-metre drag lift, but around me towered huge snow-clad peaks, the lower slopes of which were covered in old pine forest; this was snow leopard country. I quickly tired of the run, but was beckoned by the untouched powder slopes running down from a high ridge close by. Donning my skins to help me with the climb I ventured up through the forest. The trees were tall, thick and widely spaced, their rough outlines contrasting with the soft curves of the freshly fallen snow. The sky was clear and the sun sparkled from individual crystals, reminding me of the fragility of the snow. It was a classic powder day, and it seemed as though I had the entire Himalayas to myself – there was not another soul to be seen or heard anywhere.

Finally, I reached the ridge and prepared myself for the descent. Ready to go,

Fig 2 Whatever means of ascent you have used, the rewards are superb.

I realised that the powder could wait, it would not disappear; this was a special place and deserved more time of me. I sat on a nearby rock and let my mind wander, soaking up the tranquillity and dreaming of runs to come.

Suddenly, I was aware of being watched. I slowly turned to look up the ridge and there it was, only ten metres away, its long tail swaying in the cold, thin air, a beautiful snow leopard. As we stared at each other, fear began to take hold of me. I did not know how dangerous snow leopards were and, beautiful though the creature was, I was not about to satisfy its hunger. If I skied straight down from where I was, surely, even though I would have to turn to maintain control, it would not be able to follow me through the deep snow. I shot off.

Looking back, I could see it starting after me. I speeded up, barely in control. It was still gaining on me, but I dare not go any faster. Then I realised that it was not trying to catch me, but was descending on a parallel route; I had found a friend to share this great run with. Leaping clear of the snow, it would land again in an explosion of powder, emerging with another tremendous leap. Its jumps matching my turns, we descended together. I was whooping like a small child experiencing his first sledge ride; all the fear was gone and the enjoyment obviously mutual.

Sadly, all runs come to an end, even in the mighty Himalayas, and as the slope ran out I collapsed exhausted in the snow. Recovering, I turned to look for my new-found partner, but it was nowhere to be seen and looking back up the slope my tracks stood alone. At first I was puzzled and disappointed, but as I looked around again I realised that in such places anything was possible, even skiing with a snow leopard.

I have written this book in the hope that the information within its pages may help some of you to realise your own ski dreams.

Introduction

What is real snow? It is the deep bottomless powder, the exasperating breakable crust, the ankle-snapping wet crud and the smooth, creamy spring snow. It is the stuff which falls from the sky, untouched by thousands of skiers, untouched by the piste machines. It has a myriad of shapes and forms, a natural beauty, but to enjoy it intimately demands a degree of commitment not found on the piste. For the adventurous spirit the ability to ski off-piste, real skiing on real snow, can open up a whole new area of possibilities and provide endless challenges.

In the following pages I will show you how to escape the crowded pistes and show you ways to enjoy a very beautiful, natural playground, but also to respect its authority. The high mountains contain an awesome energy which must be treated with tact; too many have discovered its fickleness to their cost. The price for venturing into untracked snows can be very high, but like all great adventures the rewards can be magnificent.

Why should I encourage you into such treacherous territory? Well, it's fun, it's exhilarating, and many believe it is the ultimate in ski enjoyment to be gliding down through deep soft powder with a clear blue sky overhead. You will probably go anyway, and it is vital to go armed with the knowledge that will help to reduce the risk and with a real awareness of what that risk entails. It is also better to go with techniques that will enhance the experience. I can not make it completely safe for you, but, after all, that is not what skiing real snow is about.

So, what standard of skier do you need to be? Technically, even an intermediate skier who can barely parallel can be taught to travel off-piste, and some of the techniques I have included would be suitable for such a person. However, whether you are an intermediate or an advanced skier, I think you will find something of value within these pages. It is an attitude of mind that is the most important requirement; you need to want to escape the masses and explore a new and fresh world – explore it with an open mind and meet its many challenges with enthusiasm. If you have this adventurous free spirit then join me, read on and may the tracks you leave behind you be an expression of this freedom.

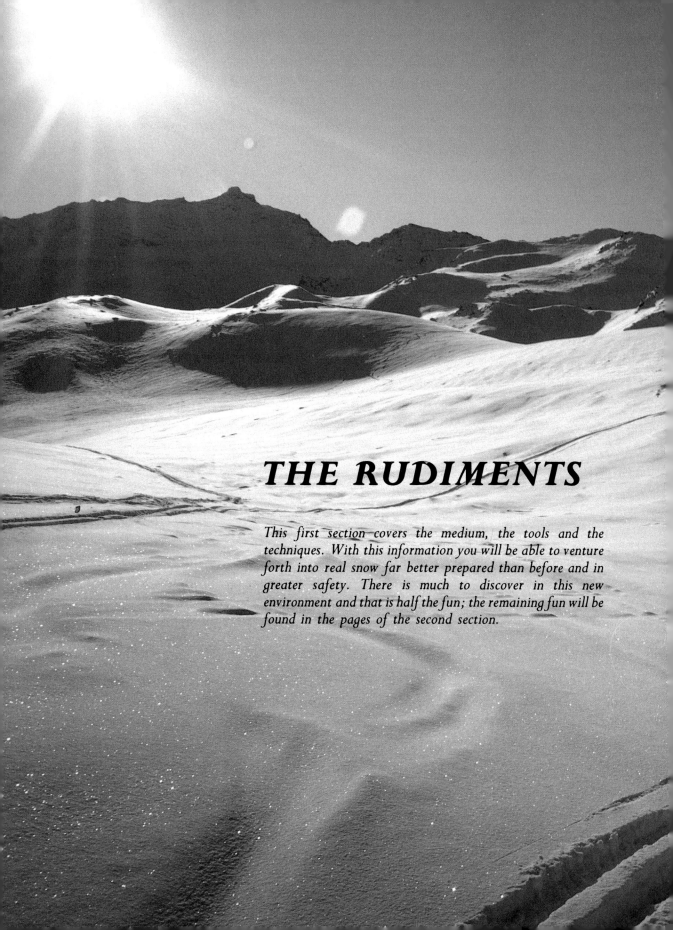

THE RUDIMENTS

This first section covers the medium, the tools and the techniques. With this information you will be able to venture forth into real snow far better prepared than before and in greater safety. There is much to discover in this new environment and that is half the fun; the remaining fun will be found in the pages of the second section.

1 The Medium

So, you have decided that this adventure might be for you; good. Let's start by trying to understand the medium we are using for our enjoyment a little better. We all know the beauty of the snowflake, each one so unique that it almost defies classification, but classify we must in order to communicate our ideas and knowledge. The International Commission on Snow and Ice uses a letter/number code to describe snow types. It has ten basic forms and is frequently supplemented by the Magano and Lee (1966) classification which has eighty categories. Clearly, as skiers we do not need such a complex understanding. We are concerned with the snow under and around our skis, how it gets there, how stable it is, and how to ski it. The following is a very simple classification which should be sufficient to meet

Fig 3 Powder snow.

these criteria. Some additional specialised forms will be added when I talk about the stability of the snowpack.

Light   Crystals which when held in your hand can be blown away (classic powder).
Heavy   This will not pass the above test and generally has a wetter feel to it (good snowball snow). Its extreme form is sometimes known as porridge!
Deep   Higher than the ankle bone and sometimes, if you are lucky and a good story teller, higher than the head bone! The term bottomless is used when there is apparently no base to the snow.
Shallow   Between the ankle bone and the ground.
Crust   Any crusty surface to the snow.

Sometimes it will break easily and consistently and at other times it will support your weight, giving way only occasionally.
Hardpack   All those surfaces that will not allow the ski to sink in at all. Hard névé and ice are typical forms.
Softpack   The edged ski will cut into this easily. This includes the beautiful and easily skied spring and corn snows.
Sastrugi   Wind sculptured snow which is usually also hardpack.

The relevance of the above classification will become evident when we examine the techniques required to ski off-piste. It can still be used, however, to help to evaluate the stability of the snowpack.

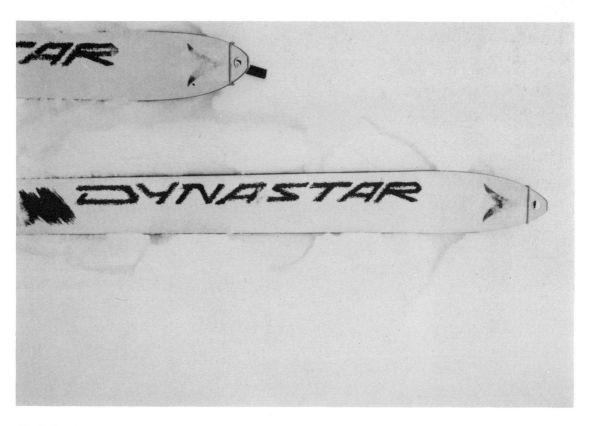

Fig 4   Crust.

Fig 5 Deep powder.

Avalanches

Avalanches are probably the single biggest danger threatening the skier of real snow. No matter how much knowledge you possess, the longer you spend in the high mountains the greater is the likelihood that you will be caught by one. A realistic appreciation of this aspect of the mountain environment is essential; avalanches can and frequently do kill. So, having issued this dire warning, what can you, the skier, do on arrival at your chosen ski area to check the avalanche potential?

Firstly, check the previous weather. The greatest hazard is during and for about 24 hours after a new fall of snow. The pisteurs or ski-patrollers will frequently

Fig 6 My partner survived a 300 metre ride in this enormous slab avalanche in the Kulu Himalayas.

14

Fig 7   The danger of the avalanche lurks everywhere; this one has come right on to the piste.

warn you of avalanche danger with signs or flags. You would be well advised to take heed of their advice, as after all they do know the area. Immediately after and sometimes during a snow storm you will hear them blasting the slopes. They are using a variety of explosive devices in an effort to release any dangerous snow slopes. Generally, they only clear those slopes that threaten the recognised ski areas. Unfortunately, we are often faced with an agonising decision: it has been snowing hard all night and then it dawns beautifully clear. Out on the slopes there is a metre of fresh new powder to tempt us. Is it safe? We can never be totally sure,

but we can reduce the odds of making the wrong decision if we follow certain procedures.

Secondly, we should check out the local knowledge. Pisteurs, ski-instructors, Guides or even local skiers will know which slopes are avalanche-prone. They may not tell you where the best powder is to be found, but they should not mind telling you which slopes to avoid.

Thirdly, on arrival at a prospective slope we can follow a number of checks:

1. Look at the surrounding slopes and if a slope of the same aspect, altitude and angle has avalanched, suspect yours and

Fig 8   An avalanche has occurred here, so we must also suspect the slope to the right.

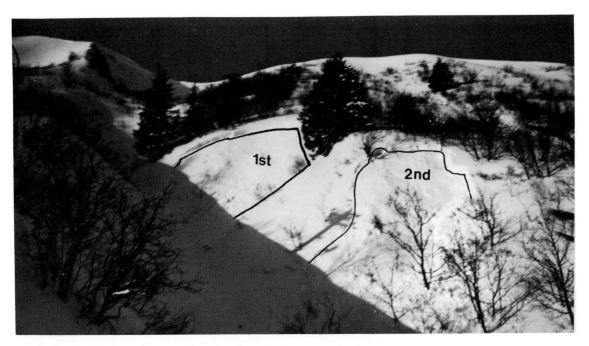

Fig 9   The slope, which has the same angle, aspect and altitude, has also avalanched.

Fig 10   Cracks. This slope and those surrounding it are extremely suspect.

choose an alternative.

2.   Look for signs of instability. Sun-balling and slumping can indicate a danger of loose snow avalanches. Cracks may be a sign of unstable slabs.

3.   Dig a snowpit and examine the snowpack.

4.   Use the ski pole test.

5.   Test ski a 'safe' slope of the same aspect, altitude and angle. A safe slope is one which is short, has an easy run-out and where the consequences of an avalanche would not be serious.

6.   Test ski the slope with the security of a rope.

7.   If you are still worried and there is no alternative, choose the safest line.

I will explain these checks in more detail later, but before you can use them to evaluate the avalanche potential an understanding of what triggers avalanches is necessary. I will try to keep the technical information to a minimum, as the references at the end of the book can be used if you have a special interest. We can divide avalanches into two major categories, loose snow and slab.

Loose Snow Avalanches

These are usually either innocuous looking sluffs or the enormous powder avalanches about which we can do nothing. Sluffs can be dangerous when they are confined to narrow gulleys, and a slope which shows evidence of sluffing should be treated with a great deal of caution. Similarly, a slope with signs of sun-balling should be treated with respect as this also indicates instability.

If you do get caught in such a sluff, if you can retain your balance it is possible to ski out of it. I remember my first encounter with a small loose snow avalanche. It was a beautifully clear day and I was skiing alone in Thyon 2000 near Verbier. The slope had been beckoning me all day but, because it required a short scramble along a ridge to reach it, had remained un-skied. Being young, foolish and having little imagination I decided to investigate. On arrival at the slope I hung on to a rock and jumped up and down to test the snow, it seemed safe so I started. It was tremendous, the powder was even deeper than I had thought it would be – when I turned round to inspect my tracks I realised with horror why. There were no tracks to be seen anywhere, just a large sluff. No wonder the powder had felt deep! I gingerly made my way back to the piste, a little shaken but much wiser. Even small sluffs can bury you; that lovely soft snow can pack like concrete when it comes to a halt. So, never be complacent about soft, light snows and never ski off-piste alone.

Slabs

Slab avalanches are a very different matter to loose snow avalanches; they are nearly always serious. There are several categories of slab, but they all release in basically the same way.

On another occasion in Thyon 2000, I was skiing with two friends. We had been skiing the same slope – good powder in the trees – all day, gradually working our way along a ridge. We chose a different line each time, and one run we decided on meant clambering down a few rocks. Clive went first, then me, closely followed by Tony. Clive moved on to the slope which was quite compact, but as I joined him there was a loud ominous crump and a crack appeared right between my feet. Clive grabbed me, but not as quickly as I grabbed Tony who was still perched on the rocks. The slope did not go, but we did – back to the piste very chastened. Anyone who has experienced the sound of a large slab cracking will know what I mean when I say it is an awesome sound. You can feel the power that is about to be released. On that occasion we were lucky and I decided that it was high time that I learned more about avalanches.

What had probably happened was that the hot sun had been warming the rocks all day and these, in turn, had melted the snow lying next to them. This meltwater then trickled down beneath the snowpack, providing a layer of lubrication for the slab above to slide upon. This is the crux of evaluating the slab avalanche potential of a particular slope: there needs to be a layer of weakness within the snowpack. This

weakness can take several forms. It can be a layer of water as described above or it can be a layer of ice or weaker snow crystals. A phenomenon known as depth hoar, which causes large fragile crystals, or graupel, pellet-like crystals are typical layers of weakness.

Another classically unstable slab is *windslab*. As its name implies, it is formed by the wind. It does not have to be snowing, because the wind can pick up any loose crystals that are lying around. The number of crystals that the wind can carry depends upon its speed; the faster the wind, the more it can carry. It follows that when the wind speed drops it will shed some of its load, and this load will consist of very broken up snowflakes because of all the battering they have received. These crystals will form into a firm cohesive slab

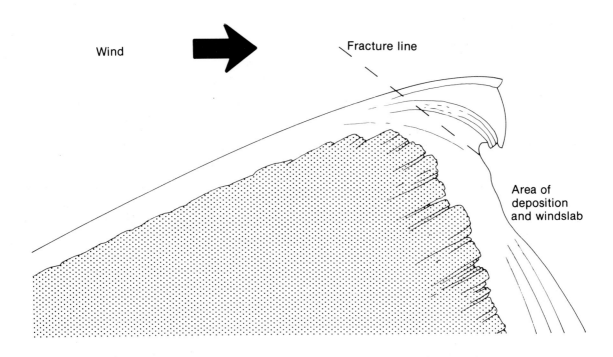

Fig 11   A cornice.

which has little adhesiveness with the underlying layers or with any subsequent layers on top.

We can recognise windslab firstly by geographical location. It will only form in areas where the wind speed is forced to drop, such as on the lee side of ridges and in hollows, and secondly by its feel and appearance. It has a milky or chalky look and is usually smooth. Windslab will often make a squeaky noise if you plant your pole in it and then rotate the pole. A lot of sastrugi on a slope indicates that the wind has been blowing hard, as it is the wind which sculptures these shapes. These slopes, the windward ones, are safe, but watch out for the leeward ones where you will almost certainly find windslab.

The Snow Profile

The best way of assessing all these factors is to examine the snow profile using a snowpit. This can be dug using a snow shovel or the tail of your ski. It should be approximately 75cm (30 inches) wide, as deep as possible and on the same slope as you intend to ski. Smooth the sides carefully using the edge of the ski as this will enable you to see the structure more clearly. Then examine the profile in a number of ways. First, using a bare finger (unless it is very cold when a gloved hand, ski pole tip or the base plate of a compass can be used) prod the snow every few centimetres (the weaknesses can be very thin). This will give you an idea of any hard or soft layers. You are looking for any marked inconsistencies; if it is to be safe, the profile should change gradually. Depth hoar will appear as a layer of larger than average crystals which feel glass-like, but which with a little more pressure on them will collapse spontaneously.

Fig 12   A snow profile; examining the layers.

Fig 13   A closer examination reveals several suspect layers.

Fig 14 Cut two oblique slots and prepare to stamp down across them.

Fig 15 Testing; by stamping down with my boot I have released a couple of layers which correspond to the layers of weakness. A very unstable layer will be released by a light stamp, or if you are using the shovel test a light pull. The ability to correlate the degree of force needed with the level of instability will only come with experience, so dig lots of profiles.

Secondly, examine all the crystals, looking again for any marked changes in their size or texture.

Finally, look at the water content of the various layers. Free running water or very wet layers will act as lubricants for the snow above. If the pit reaches right down to the ground, examine that too. Grass or smooth rocks will obviously allow the snow above to slide more easily than, for example, a scree slope.

Having inspected the pit, there are two further checks you can make. Using the tail of the ski cut two oblique channels down the back of the pit and then stamp

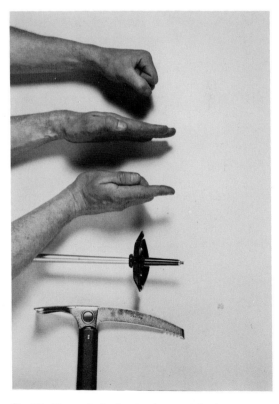

Fig 16 To evaluate the hardness of the layers more accurately you can grade the ease of penetration of the following: (i) fist; (ii) four fingers; (iii) one finger; (iv) end of ski pole; (v) end of the ice-axe pick. Be wary when low numbers are next to high numbers.

down with the other ski across these two channels. If a slab slides away it is a good indication that the same will happen if you ski the slope. A similar check, which is probably better if you are carrying a snow shovel of the flat variety (the curved models, though good for digging, do not do this test very well), is to cut the same two channels as before and then to insert the shovel perpendicularly between the two cuts and to pull outwards horizontally, applying no leverage. If a slab is released by this action, you should suspect the slope. These slabs need to be at least 10 to 15cm (4 to 6 inches) thick to be of any concern; anything less can be skied with little trouble.

Digging pits every time you change slope can be very time-consuming, and a quicker though less informative method is to use the ski pole. Push the pole as far into the snow as possible; this may take several attempts. When you have a hole of some depth, move the pole in a circular fashion to create a conical hole which will allow you to check the profile. As you withdraw the pole, use the basket to feel for any layering in much the same way as you did with your finger. I frequently use this method when I am going uphill on a tour. Having first established a clear idea of what the profile is like by using a pit, I can then constantly monitor the slope as I ascend. Another on-the-move indicator is to watch what happens to the snow under your skis: if it is breaking away from your tracks then, again, be wary.

Test-ski a Safe Slope

The next procedure is to test-ski a safe slope of the same aspect, altitude and angle. Ideally you need a small slope where the consequences of a release will not harm either you or any other skiers in the area. You must try to stress the slope by skiing it vigorously. The reason for this is that just because a slope has supported one skier there is no guarantee that it will support others. This is a very important point, since as soon as a slope sports one set of tracks then everybody follows with abandon. Unfortunately, it is impossible to define how many tracks are needed to indicate whether a slope is safe or not, as every slope is so different. Also, the temperature variations within the snow-pack can cause its structure to change fairly quickly, so even slopes that have been skied should be checked.

Before you start test-skiing slopes, I would suggest that you serve an apprenticeship under the watchful eye of either a

Fig 17   The ski pole test.

qualified ski-instructor or a UIAGM approved Mountain Guide. The French insist that only people with the latter qualification should be allowed to teach away from the main ski areas, which are usually defined as those areas where there are glaciers. Do be careful when employing a 'ski guide'; some have neither of the above qualifications and just being a good skier is not enough. The judgement required for decisions made away from the piste demands considerable experience.

If you are in the middle of a ski tour and are uncertain about a slope but have no alternative, then you could test-ski it with the protection of a rope to which you are belayed via a solid anchor. (I will cover belaying in depth in Chapter 7.) As before, test the slope vigorously. If it does go, then you can descend down the avalanche track in relative safety, but continue to watch out for the slope on either side and above. If you do not have a rope in the party then you will have to choose the safest line.

Choosing the Safest Line

It is very difficult to generalise as to which is the safest line, but these few guidelines may help. Fortunately, the easiest and most efficient route is often the safest. Stick to either shallow or very steep slopes, as avalanches usually occur on slopes around 30 degrees (although they

Fig 18   Test-skiing a slope protected by a rope.

have been recorded on slopes of as little as 12 degrees). On slopes over 50 degrees the snow rarely adheres long enough to be a threat, but these slopes are too steep for most of us to adhere to as well! Wind-scoured ridges, although often unpleasant to ski, are usually safe. Tree-lined slopes are safer than open ones, but avalanches can still occur on them. Choose slopes that

have good run-outs on them and not ones which go over cliffs or into culs-de-sac or crevassed terrain.

If you have to traverse a dangerous slope, as leader you should choose an angle which necessitates using your poles to push you along. If you go any steeper, the people behind you who are sliding on your packed tracks will be going too fast. It is

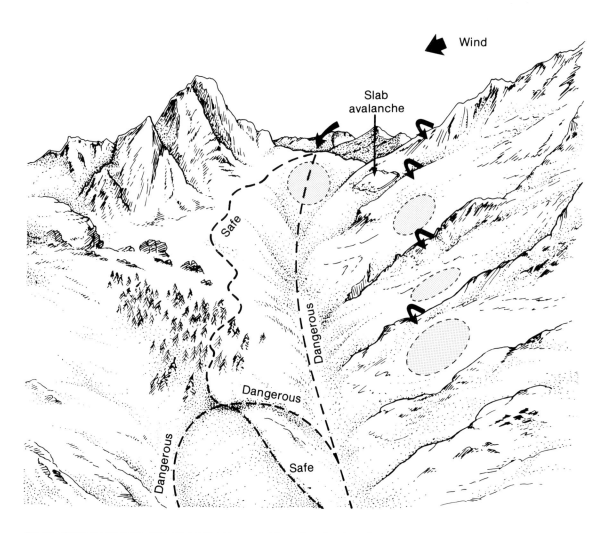

Fig 19 Typical safe route. The wind will eddy around the ridges forming other areas of instability. We must suspect all the slopes of the same angle, aspect, and altitude (these are indicated by the areas of shading). The safe route follows a shelf, avoiding the valley which could channel any releases, and then continues along a ridge instead of plunging back into the valleys.

important to cross the danger zone one at a time and when you reach safety look back at your companions so that if the slope does go you can see where they disappeared.

In dire circumstances it would be wise to cover your nose and mouth with a Balaclava or scarf to prevent them becoming blocked by the snow. Many victims die from hypothermia so again, in very serious situations, ensure you are wearing extra clothing. The problem of whether to remove your skis under these conditions and walk is a very difficult one. On the one hand your skis will cut a ready-made fracture line and on the other you may, by walking, cut a dangerously deep trough. The chances of skiing out of a slab avalanche are very slim indeed and it is more likely that your skis and poles will drag you further under. Certainly, remove your hands from the straps as this will enable you to cover your face if you do get caught.

Emergency Procedures

If you get swept away by an avalanche what can you do to increase your chances of survival? Some you can ski out of, but in others, particularly the deep slabs, this would be very difficult. If you decide to try, then use the techniques described later for skiing deep heavy snow, and at the same time keep looking for escape routes. However, only the very best and very cool skiers are likely to be able to cope, and even they would need a large element of luck. Alternatively, you should try to delay your departure by thrusting your poles into the substrata or leaping up the slope. Any tactic that will help you get near to the top of the avalanche is a good thing.

Once caught in an avalanche the best advice is to try to stay on the surface using a swimming action. Once, high in the Kulu Himalayas, my partner was caught in a huge avalanche. He remained aware of his surroundings and by a rolling action not only managed to stay on the surface but also avoided being swept over some enormous ice cliffs. I have heard of several reports praising this rolling action; in fact, a Frenchman, for a price, has offered to demonstrate the technique! As the avalanche grinds to a halt make a last desperate effort to reach the surface. Anything that protrudes will aid your discovery by rescuers. As you are engulfed cover your face and try to maintain a breathing space. Try not to panic and conserve your energy; shouting for help will probably be ineffective at this stage. An analysis of Alpine avalanche statistics shows that after two hours of burial only twenty per cent of the victims survived.

Clearly, it is essential that any witnesses to an accident act swiftly. You will be shocked, but, although speed is vital, make sure that the slope is safe before commencing a search. If there are no further dangers proceed to the point where you last saw the victim and mark the spot with your ski pole. Your search should take on two phases; the first is a rapid search of the area looking for obvious signs like the skis, clothing or poles. This search should take place no matter how close at hand the rescue services are. If, however, it draws a blank and if, and *only* if, the rescue services are very close by should you leave the site and inform them. If they are some distance away, proceed with a more thorough search which should take the following form. Using the tails of your skis or your ski poles (you can get special poles that screw together for this purpose) probe the

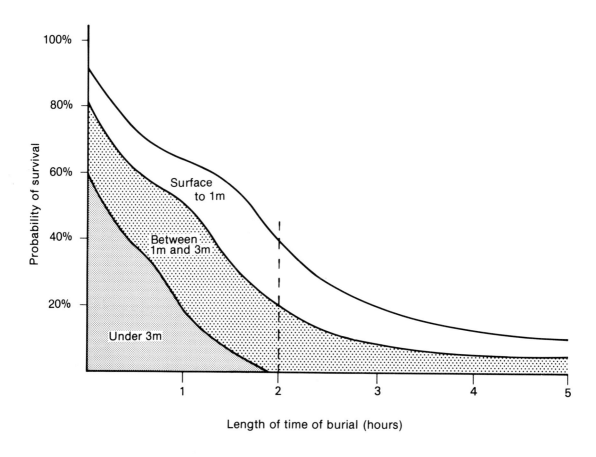

Fig 20 Survival time in an avalanche. The chances of survival diminish rapidly after a couple of hours regardless of the depth of burial.

debris in an ordered pattern. With each probe site 70cm (27 inches) apart, work systematically over the whole area. As you can imagine this is not a very satisfactory solution, but by the time the rescue personnel arrive the victim's chances of survival will have been reduced considerably. For this same reason the various devices on the market that aid location by the rescue services are only really of value if the accident occurs within easy reach of them.

Party Precautions

The only satisfactory solution, besides not getting caught in the first place, is for each member of the party to carry a transceiver. This is a small device that emits a signal on a specific frequency; the two most commonly used are 457Khz and 2275Khz. The advantage of this device is that it can also receive a signal which is changed into an audio one that varies in intensity according to the proximity of the transmitter. There is one particular device being developed which uses a liquid quartz

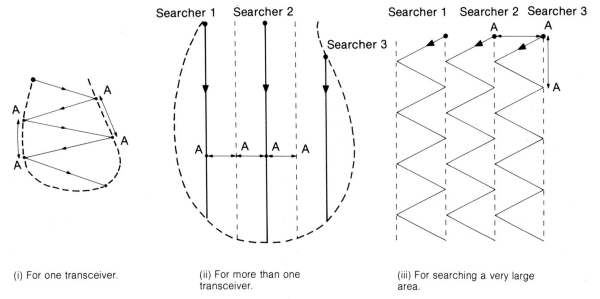

(i) For one transceiver.

(ii) For more than one transceiver.

(iii) For searching a very large area.

Fig 21   Using a transceiver. (a) Search patterns. Distance AA must be within the range of the transceiver, once a signal has been received proceed with a fine search. If you are only looking for one body, turn the other devices off once a signal has been picked up.

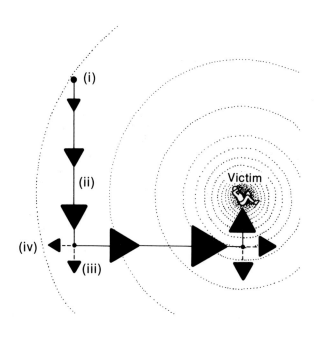

Fig 22   Using a transceiver.
(b) Fine searching.
(i) Orientate the transceiver to the strongest signal and walk in that direction.
(ii) As the signal increases turn down the volume.
(iii) Continue until the signal diminishes, turn 180 degrees and return to the point where the signal was strongest.
(iv) Turn 90 degrees and if the signal diminishes after walking a short distance turn 180 degrees and repeat the whole process until you can pinpoint the victim. This needs practice and you must stick to this procedure rigidly; do not be tempted to take short-cuts, as it will usually take longer!

display to give a visual response. The sets are available in either single or dual frequencies and there is much debate as to which is the best. The International Commission for Alpine Rescue, IKAR, report that the 457Khz frequency is significantly faster and more accurate. However, despite the wishes of the Commission, it is unlikely that this frequency will be adopted world-wide. The Austrians, for example, already have some quarter of a million sets of the 2275Khz variety in use, and the Americans report considerable interference on the 457Khz band from Trident submarines. I suggest that it would be wise to buy a dual frequency set.

When using a transceiver, follow the pattern in Figs 21 & 22. As the signal gets louder turn the setting down, because the ear can detect changes in volume more clearly at lower levels. With practice it is possible to search large areas quickly and thoroughly, but it does take practice.

If you decide to use transceivers there are two golden rules to follow. The first is that they must be worn beneath substantial clothing so that they cannot become detached from your person. The second is that they must be switched on at the start of the day and checked to see that they are transmitting and they must be left on until you arrive safely at your destination. Turning them on intermittently, only

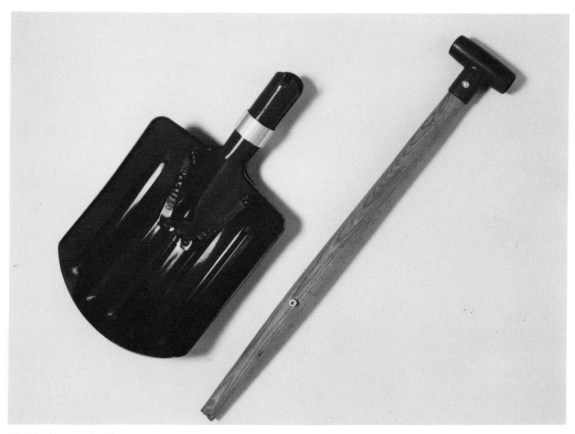

Fig 23   A snow shovel.

when you think you might need them, is just courting disaster. Some models have a battery check built into them, but for those that do not you will need to follow the manufacturer's recommendations regarding battery life. If in doubt, change them, and if you are going on a tour make sure you carry enough spares.

On location of the victim it will be necessary to dig them out as quickly as possible, and there is no question that a proper snow shovel is invaluable in these circumstances.

IKAR are testing a variety of other systems, including a method developed by the Norwegians called *Suchwinkel* which uses dowsing rods and which, in spite of much scepticism, has achieved some very convincing results. Finally, they have also been testing a gas-filled balloon which, when inflated, will lift you to the surface of the avalanche. Again, demonstrations have been impressive.

It would be unrealistic to ignore the information contained in this chapter. We all hope it will not happen to us, and with some of this knowledge we should be able to load the odds in our favour. I hope I have not put you off: awareness is half the battle in reducing hazards to an acceptable level.

2 The Tools

There are many misconceptions in the clothing and equipment world, and in this chapter I have tried to clear up many of these, as well as passing on hints and tips that I have picked up over the years.

Clothing

Several years ago, while teaching a group of skiers, it became clear to me after the first couple of runs that all but one were good parallel skiers. She was just inconsistent; the occasional skilful turn mixed in with a number of hesitant turns resulted in a rather disappointing performance. Her skiing ability, plus a mixture of very dated and drab clothing made her very self-conscious, which did not help. We persisted for a couple of days, but with no real improvements. One evening we all went to a bar and on the way passed a ski shop, in the window of which was an attractive one-piece ski suit. 'Are these one-piece suits very practical?' she asked. I replied that I was very happy with the one that I used. The next day she turned up sporting the suit and the transformation to her skiing was remarkable. It was not the practical nature of the suit that caused this change, but rather the way she felt in it: she knew she looked good.

I am not suggesting that you all go out and buy a new outfit every time your skiing hits a plateau, and it does sound rather superficial to say that the way we look should affect our performance, but I do believe that it is an important factor. An average skier's time down a slalom course might well be bettered if he wore racing pants and a racing jumper. The reasons for this are complex, but relate to a technique that I will be discussing later known as visualisation. Many of you will probably protest vehemently 'that this does not apply to you, and it may not. I know a number of skiers who need to dress down to feel comfortable. The point is that you must feel good about what you are wearing, both mentally and physically, and it must be appropriate for the task.

On the practical side there are a number of important points about clothing which will affect your performance. You are operating in a very hostile environment, and, as you well know, it is not all sunny days and clear blue skies. The temperature can easily drop to minus 20°C (-4°F); add to this any wind and the wind-chill factor will reduce it still further. Your body must be protected from these extremes of temperature so that it can perform the highly skilful tasks asked of it in safety.

At the same time the clothing must not restrict movement, and this is the first dilemma that the designer has to face up to. All warm clothing relies on trapping dead air, as this offers the highest degree of insulation. If the clothing is too loose, you will move this dead air as you move around, thus destroying some of its insulative value. Conversely, if it is too tight it will restrict your circulation which in turn will make your extremities cold.

For this reason, my ideal clothing system is based on the principle that it must be well tailored. It will fit closely around the main body, usually with a belt or elastic waistband. The arms, shoulders and legs will allow a full range of movement without disturbing the main bodice and the air trapped inside it.

When you try on clothing make sure that you try on the whole system and put it through the complete range of movements you are likely to make when skiing. For example, if you are buying a separate jacket and pants, try them both on at the same time. There is nothing worse than finding that when you bend over the small of your back is bared. It is very important to keep this area protected as it is the place where your kidneys, which carry a lot of blood, are closest to the surface. In fact, some motor cyclists wear a kidney belt, which is a broad band of extra insulation, around their midriffs. Whether such a device could be designed for the skier, who is obviously more mobile, I do not know. Perhaps a scarf tied around the waist would be as good.

A one-piece suit tends to solve this problem, but whether it is better than a combination is a difficult question. I have been skiing in a one-piecer for many years and I find it ideal for all but the very warmest of conditions. Providing you can unzip the front you can regulate the temperature quite well, and the value of a one-piecer in the powder speaks for itself. Having said that, however, remember that any snow that does get down your neck will have to travel the whole length of your body before it can escape, by which time it is cold water. A two-piece system is certainly more versatile, and when I am ski touring, which involves climbing uphill, I use such a system.

Basic Design Features

Whether you adopt a one- or two-piece system there are some basic design features to look for. The collar should be large enough to allow your head to be encased up to the level of your mouth and perhaps as far as your nose. I have always found this feature far more satisfactory than a scarf, although many people do use scarves, particularly the silk ones which the snow does not stick to. I do not favour hoods that I cannot detach, because when I fall over it fills up with snow and then it seems impossible to empty it without it going down your neck. The system I prefer is a thin windproof nylon hood which is stored within the collar of the garment. I then wear a normal ski hat, and in the same compartment as the hood I store a motor cyclist's silk Balaclava for when the temperatures are really cold. Inside the collar I like a second elasticated collar which sits snugly and comfortably around my neck and prevents those cold snowflakes from getting inside.

Moving on down the body, I would like to see someone design an integrated glove system where the glove and the sleeve could be joined together. Cold hands can make you feel miserable even when everything else is marvellous. There are two main reasons for cold hands: the first is that the gloves are often too tight, hampering circulation, and the second is that they do not adequately protect the wrist, where the blood supply is closest to the surface. An integrated system would not only help the second point, but would also prevent the snow from collecting in the wrist area after a fall. Mitts are unquestionably warmer than gloves, but personally I prefer the dexterity offered by gloves, unless it is very cold. Whichever you decide upon, ensure that they are big enough and that they cover the wrist. I often sew a Velcro band around the wrist and on the inside of my sleeves to make my own integrated system. Whenever you have to take your gloves off in cold conditions put them inside your jacket rather than on the ground or on the top of your ski pole, and just before putting them back on blow into them a couple of times – it is like putting on toasted gloves!

Any zips should have good covering flaps to prevent snow sticking to them and the wind blowing through them. I like to have a number of pockets in which to store things, and I find the large cargo style pockets, out of harm's way on the legs, especially useful. These pockets must have adequate zips and covers otherwise they just become collectors of snow. Velcro has limited uses as a fastening system on ski clothing because it very easily becomes clogged with snow; for this reason it should not be the only method employed.

Extra padding on the knees is very much appreciated on long chair-lift rides where the knees can become very stiff with the cold. Additional waterproofing on the seat is also welcomed on those wet chairs. What has happened to those little pockets that used to appear on the arms that we could keep our lift passes in? I hate having the thing dangling around my neck, threatening to strangle me as it spins in the wind, and I don't feel confident about the security of the plastic pouches that you can slip over the arm. A lost lift ticket can cause enormous problems. There are a number of different systems to be found at the bottom of the trouser legs, which, as long as they are robust, keep out the snow, fit over the top of the boot and do not restrict leg movement when they are in place, should be fine.

If I am wearing a combination of jacket and trousers then I always prefer salopettes. They help to eliminate any chilling around the kidney area and avoid the problem of separation between the jacket and the trousers. Personally, I don't like racing pants as I find them too cold in many conditions and a little restrictive; on the other hand they do give a lot of sensory feedback about what the legs are doing, which some people like. If you like them and are warm enough in them, then wear them.

Materials

Of all the insulative materials available, the best is still natural down. The problem is that it is very expensive and if it gets wet it becomes a soggy mass with little insulative value. Many of the synthetic equivalents are close to down in performance, and since a new one appears every season I can only suggest that you compare the clo values. A clo is a unit representing the insulative value of a material.

For the outer skin we can choose between cottons, nylons and the revolutionary breathable waterproof fabrics. I have found the latter to be excellent at their best and at their worst no worse than anything else. It is important not to expect too much from them and to remember that they need careful handling. When they become dirty they will not work so well, and in some cold conditions any condensation will freeze thereby blocking the pores through which the water vapour would normally pass. If you do sweat in them, it is probably because you are wearing too many clothes; if the body is too hot it will sweat in order to lose some of this excessive heat. Remember, they do not prevent you from sweating, they just allow the water vapour to escape thus reducing the build-up of condensation. If you do choose a garment made of one of these breathable waterproof fabrics be sure that all the seams are taped, otherwise they will leak annoyingly. Many manufacturers have started to use cotton fabrics again, but generally they are no cheaper and do not appear to have any great advantages over other materials. Bearing in mind these criteria, the rest is up to you and the designer's imagination.

Underwear has also undergone some radical changes; string vests and itchy woollen long johns are things of the past. The new breed of underwear will draw the sweat away from the skin, reducing that clammy feeling. These new polypropylene-based materials are certainly an improvement and most people find them very comfortable. However, wool is still one of the best insulators, and, if you really suffer from the cold, you can buy woollen vests and long johns which are much improved from the itchy things of the past.

Glasses and Goggles

Before moving on to the hardware of boots, bindings and skis, let me first say a word about glasses and goggles. They are essential items and should be worn at all times on the mountains. Too many people do not wear them, presumably for reasons of vanity. Even when there are clouds about, the dangerous ultraviolet rays are still getting through and the damage they do is permanent. Whether you wear glasses or goggles is up to you. I tend to wear glasses until the weather is very bad, and then I find goggles better.

Double lenses do not seem to mist up as badly as single ones, and a useful tip is to carry a piece of lint on to which you have sprinkled a small amount of washing-up liquid. Periodically wipe the lens, inside and out, and this should prevent any further misting. Some goggles sport different coloured lenses that are supposed to enhance visibility when it is bad, and some certainly seem to do so. The best advice I can give is to try them and see which works best for you.

Boots

Downhill Boots

Downhill ski boots come in two designs: front entry and rear entry. The pros and cons for each are numerous and tend to be very personal, so let me first outline some basics which hold true regardless of the design.

Comfort should be your biggest priority when choosing a boot. Uncomfortable feet can ruin an otherwise perfect day, not to mention the detrimental effect they will have on your skiing. A bad workman blames his tools the old saying goes, but if it is painful for the master craftsman even to hold his chisel then how can he possibly carve accurately with it? The same applies to skiing: sensitivity in your feet leads to sensitivity in your skiing. Feet that are constantly in discomfort cannot concentrate on giving you the feedback you require to ski well.

With most modern boots it is only necessary to wear one pair of socks and on very cold days these can be supplemented by very thin polypropylene inner socks. The boot should fit firmly around the heel and ankle, but be loose enough round the toes to allow them to wriggle about. This is important in order that the circulation is not impaired, thus causing cold feet. When you try on a pair of boots the following may help you choose the correct fitting:

1.   Do the boot up completely and stand in them as though you were skiing, with your shin bones resting against the tongues of the boot. This ensures that your heel slides to the back of the boot, and if you don't do this the boot will often appear to be too small and be cramping the toes.
2.   In the warmth of the shop your feet will probably have swollen more than they would when skiing, so try the boots on with either a very thin pair of socks or no socks at all.
3.   Put on a pair of skis if possible and go through the motions of skiing for several minutes. This should highlight any likely painful spots. It will also entertain the other customers, but at least you will be sure of the comfort of your boots.

Ski shops the world over have improved dramatically in the last few years in the quality of the service they offer, and most will do an excellent job of ensuring your comfort.

A good ski boot will have very little flex laterally or backwards, but should flex forwards. This forward flex is absolutely vital. Jump up and down a few times trying to land as softly as possible, noticing how the ankle bends. Now try the same thing with your ankles stiff. Convinced? Several years ago a major boot manufacturer produced a model that was, because of its comfort, very popular. Gradually, however, ski-instructors began to notice that these boots caused the user's skiing to be noticeably wooden, simply because the boots were too stiff. Even racers were cutting the boots about to improve the

forward flex. Fortunately, the company has redesigned the boot, incorporating a good forward flex system.

Boots that have a variable flex system are good, because in the warmth of the shop the plastic will be soft but it will probably have a different flex pattern when used in the sub-zero temperatures on snow. Some skiers will also want to change the flex pattern according to the type of skiing they are doing. Personally, I like a soft flexing boot for off-piste, as I feel that it allows your balance to adapt to the ever-changing terrain more easily.

A modern boot has a number of other adjustments. The forward lean angle of the boot can often be adjusted and this is quite different to the forward flex. When we bend our ankles forward, moving our shin bones towards our toes, we make the whole of our foot more stable laterally, and this can be an advantage when we are trying to control an edged ski. The boot can help by allowing some forward flexing, but also by having a degree of permanent lean built into the design. The amount you use is a matter of personal preference, but I would try to use as little as possible providing you can flex your boot easily – what feels right probably is right. There are some notable ski teachers who argue that we should have very little forward lean in order to allow a much looser style to develop. This is certainly true of the ski racer who often has to glide on a flat ski to maintain speed, but for the skier of real snow it only applies to what are known as surf turns. I will expand on this idea further in Chapter 3.

The other major adjustment is what Jean-Claude Killy, one of the most successful ski racers of all time, called the 'secret weapon': canting. For many years, I was a sceptic, arguing that when skiing our legs are never static and that they would adapt to slight misalignments. Then I bought a pair of boots with a canting facility and, without checking, I put them on and walked out to meet my ski class. Even while walking out I realised that something was wrong and as soon as I started to ski I felt in total sympathy with my class of beginners. How do we control these planks on the ends of our legs? On inspection I discovered that my boots had been canted, so at the first opportunity I rapidly adjusted them to a neutral position. If canting can work negatively in this way, it follows that it can also work positively for those who need it. The amount of canting is quite difficult to assess, even with the aid of a canting machine. I suggest you use such a machine as a starting point and then adjust your boots until you find the position with which you are happiest. Your ski-instructor should also be able to give you good advice.

When we buy expensive boots, we are paying not only for the aforementioned facilities but also for the ability to customise the boot to our foot. This is usually achieved through some sort of foaming system and the facility for customisation is a major breakthrough in boot comfort.

Another major breakthrough is in the type of footbeds available. Most ski shops are able to supply custom-made footbeds for your boots through a variety of systems, and I believe the extra expense is well worthwhile. A number of years ago I damaged my foot and for several years could not stand for more than about an hour in my ski boots, even with footbeds in them. I tried everything until a friend recommended that I consult a podiatrician (chiropodist). After videoing me in action, taking X-rays, plaster-casts of my legs and many other things, he, in conjunction with an American company, produced an orthotic footbed which, although expensive at the time, has completely solved the problem and given me trouble-free skiing for five years. If you have a persistent foot problem this course of action may offer a solution.

For many years there has been an argument on the merits of rear versus front entry boots. To my mind, the major difficulty with the rear entry design has been in coping with the problems of different forefoot shapes. If the boots did not fit your foot shape there was very little facility to change the profile. The latest ranges of rear entry boots are much better in this respect, however, and with modern advancements in design these boots should gain in popularity. The main advantage in front entry boots is their ability to be adjusted throughout the boot's length. Rear entry boots do have one major advantage however: if you undo the back of the boot it is much more comfortable to walk in. Many ski tourers have started to use them, especially those who go in search of good skiing rather than good climbing.

Ski Touring Boot

Most touring boots are a compromise between a ski boot and a mountaineering boot, and, like so many compromises, it is rare to get the best of both worlds and more common to get the worst. Despite this, there have been a number of recent models that have been very good. As ski touring has gained in popularity so more time and energy has been spent on giving us, the customers, what we want: a ski boot that is also good for climbing or a climbing boot that can be used for skiing.

There are several new boots on the market that sport all the adjustment facilities of the downhill boots, and I think it is only a matter of time before we see a rear entry downhill boot with a Vibram climbing sole. Whichever boot you choose the major criterion must again be comfort, only this time it must be for both going downhill and uphill.

Skis

Choosing Your Skis

It is important to have the right ski for a particular type of skiing, and the criteria for choosing an off-piste ski are as varied as those for a piste ski. A ski that is good in light powder, for example, will not be very good on hard névé. Generally, however, the majority of off-piste conditions do favour a softer flexing ski. This tends to be more forgiving in the varied conditions met away from the prepared runs, and a soft shovel can be a help in allowing the tip of the ski to float to the surface in deeper snows. If you aspire to ski steep terrain the superior holding power of a stiffer ski will be a definite advantage. This ski will also have a similar advantage on hard icy surfaces where the soft ski will be very unnerving. Shorter than normal skis are certainly easier to turn in difficult snows, but can put you at a serious disadvantage if there are long schusses involved. Several years ago I was invited to observe the French Guides undergo their ski touring training at the Ecole Nationale de Ski et Alpinism in Chamonix. I spent the week on a pair of short ski-mountaineering skis which were fine in the powder and the crud, but when we had to schuss down the Vallée Blanche I was left embarrassingly far

behind and no amount of national pride, skating and pushing with my poles would allow me to catch them!

Since most of you will be skiing on-piste as well as in real snow I would recommend that you do not buy a specialised powder ski but stick initially to the skis you enjoy using on the prepared snow; you will be able to handle them off-piste as well. My own preference is for one of the high performance recreational skis which seem to be good all-round performers. They usually have a softer tip and tail, a good stiff mid-section to help the ski grip the ice, and a lively feel to them. The side cut will lie somewhere between that of the slalom ski and giant slalom ski and they should be skied at about 10 to 15 cm (4 to 6 inches) above head height. When deciding on the length of a ski look at the manufacturer's recommendations; it will be designed to be skied at a particular length relative to your ability, style and body size, and nothing will be gained by skiing it any shorter.

When choosing skis for touring you are faced not only with hundreds of downhill skis but also with a selection of specialist touring skis as well. These often have broader shovels to help the ski plane to the surface and a hole in the tip, which I always assumed was for clipping a karabiner into in times of need. I am now in doubt about this as the only time I have been in such need I found the hole too small. The skis are usually built robustly, although many piste skis nowadays also sport the tougher P-tex 2000 bases. At the tail you will often find a small notch, which has been cut there to help hold certain skin systems in place. This is easy to file out yourself if your skis do not have such a feature. Finally, the top surface is usually brightly coloured to help you find your ski when it comes off in the deep snow. I wonder how long it will be before a device is on the market which can be fixed on to the ski and used with our avalanche transceivers to aid the ski's recovery in powder.

To make this awkward choice you must first decide whether your interest will be with traditional touring, where the main concern is to use the ski to travel in the high mountains, or with the slightly more recent idea of using touring skills to reach better skiing. If it is the former you will want to choose a ski that is slightly shorter and therefore easier to carry, whereas if it is the latter you will need a ski capable of performing well.

Fig 24 A P-tex candle; hold the candle at an angle for a fast drip.

Care of Your Skis

Whichever skis you have, they are looked after in the same way. Repairing and maintaining your own skis is not a difficult task, and it is very important that you make any necessary repairs swiftly and efficiently. If you put a hole in the base of your skis that goes through to the material underneath the P-tex, it is essential that you seal this hole before water can enter. If water does enter it might freeze, delaminating the sole in the process. You can temporarily plug the hole in two ways. Firstly you can rub wax into the gap; this is very temporary but will at least keep the water out for a while. Secondly, and more permanently, using a lighted P-tex candle drip molten P-tex into the hole. It may be necessary to clean the hole of any debris and wax and, if the hole is very big, to build the repair up in layers. This repair will be quite messy and full of dirty-looking carbon deposits, but you can always do a more professional repair when you return home. Keep an eye on the

Fig 25 A P-tex candle; hold the candle horizontally for a slow drip.

Fig 26 Using a metal scraper, clear away any excess P-tex.

Fig 27   Flat-filing the base.

Fig 28   Filing the edges.

Fig 29   Checking the edges; notice the sliver of nail.

repair; sometimes, usually because the sole is full of wax, the repair does not stick. If this happens you will have to clean the sole with a de-waxer first and then do the repair again. Let the repair cool completely, then, using a metal scraper, level the P-tex down to the ski base.

At the end of the season you can clean out all these messy repairs, de-wax the sole and renew the P-tex repair. The cleanest way of doing this is to use a P-tex gun or a very hot iron to melt the P-tex; you can also buy it in thinner strip-form which is easier to melt. Having melted it in, continue as before. If the hole is very large it may be necessary to glue a slab of P-tex into place using Araldite or a similar adhesive and then fill in the gaps with melted P-tex.

Keeping your edges sharp is as important to the off-piste skier as it is to the piste skier. Obviously the edges will make no difference in powder, but on hardpack and ice sharp edges are essential. I blunt the edges for about 20 cm (8 inches) from either end on the inside and a little further on the outside edge. This makes the skis left- and right-footed, so remember to mark them as such. The exact amount to blunt them can only really be determined by trial and error. The purpose of blunting the edges is to stop the front hooking into the turns and to prevent the back from catching at the end of a turn. I sharpen each edge differently to lessen the chances of the uphill ski catching.

Take the trouble to buy a good quality file and a file card to clean it with. Any single cross-cut file will do, but look at the end of the file to check it is not twisted – cheap ones often are. Only file on the forward stroke, lifting the file clear as you return to the start; this will prolong the life of your file considerably, as it is only designed to cut on the forward stroke. Steel has a grain similar to that in wood, and you will achieve a much better result if you stroke with the grain. To determine which way the grain goes, file in both directions: one should feel smoother and produce a cleaner-looking surface, although much will depend upon the quality of the metal used. If you can't tell, don't worry, just sharpen the edges from the tip to the tail.

The base of the ski must be flat-filed to ensure that the ski is not railed, in other words that the edges are not proud of the base. Ideally you should do one edge at a time stroking from the centre of the ski outwards, thus stopping any of the swarf (the metal shavings) from becoming embedded in the base. This, however, is quite difficult, so alternatively just make sure that you brush the swarf away frequently. Check the flatness with a straight edge; your metal scraper should suffice.

Having flat-filed the base, turn the ski on to its side and sharpen the edges. You can buy a number of devices that will help you to ensure that the edges are sharpened at 90 degrees. When you have finished sharpening them, use a stone to run along the edges just to take away any burrs that are present. To check whether the edge is sharp enough, I scrape the top surface of my nail across the edge and if a thin sliver is left on the metal then I know it is right. I now use some low-grade wet and dry (emery cloth) wrapped around a block to rub down the sole, which prepares it for waxing.

There are basically two types of wax: hot wax which, as its name implies, is applied in a molten form, and cold rub-on waxes. The latter come in a variety of colours which indicate the temperatures at which they should be used and they are

Fig 30   Hot waxing; ironing in the wax.

Fig 31   Scraping the wax away with a plastic scraper.

Fig 32   The final buff with a cork.

simply rubbed on to the running surface of the ski. The former also comes suited to different temperatures, but for most uses the universal grade seems to be adequate. For many years I used to argue that I went quite fast enough without having to resort to waxes to gain speed. The point that I missed was that wax not only allows the skis to glide downhill more easily but also to glide around corners more easily, and we spend most of our time trying to ski round corners.

The waxing system I use is a universal hot wax supplemented with an appropriate rub-on wax when the temperature reaches either of the extremes and the skis begin to stick. The P-tex base is a porous surface and as such will absorb quite a lot of wax. Using an old domestic iron I melt the wax on to the surface of the ski and then literally iron it in, adding more wax if the base absorbs all that is present. You must never let the iron rest in one spot, but keep it moving gradually over the surface. The base will get quite hot and the ski will take on reverse camber, but providing you keep the iron moving you should not do any damage to the ski. When the P-tex will absorb no more wax, let the ski cool.

Once the wax has cooled you can start scraping it. Using the plastic scraper, clear away all the surface wax, especially the wax that has dripped on to the edges. Then, buff up the surface with a cork to get a really good finish and the ski will be ready to use. In soft snow conditions this type of hot-waxing can last up to a week. Providing you scrape the base thoroughly you can wax your touring skis in the same way; the skins will still stick.

At the end of the season hot-wax your skis and store them without scraping them down, making sure that the wax covers the edges so that they will not rust.

Bindings

The advice for normal piste bindings is simple: buy the best you can afford. The top models of every range are all very good, and are probably as safe as each other. Each has a slightly different functional capability – one design will release better with one type of fall, whilst another will be best in a different type of situation; but what type of fall causes the most injuries off-piste I do not know. Whichever model you choose, it must be correctly adjusted according to the manufacturer's recommendations. If you are hiring remember that the shop will generally only adjust what is known as the pre-tension. In other words, they will fit your boot to the binding, but they will not adjust the tension to suit you – that is your responsibility. There are a couple of quick and easy tests that you can do that will at least tell you whether the binding will release in the event of a fall:

1. *The toe-piece* Check that when the boot is in position there is sufficient space to be able to slide a credit card between the sole of the boot and the anti-friction pad (which must also be in good condition). If you cannot do this, raise the toe-piece by rotating the large screw on top until you can. Remove the boot and see if you can rotate the toe-piece using one hand. Your wrist strength is proportional to your ankle strength, so if you cannot do this the binding is set too tightly. To adjust it, rotate the large screw at the end of the binding; this will move the cursor inside the window on top of the binding. The higher the number, the tighter the binding, so adjust it until you can only just release it. If you have the setting too low, the binding will pre-release and you will

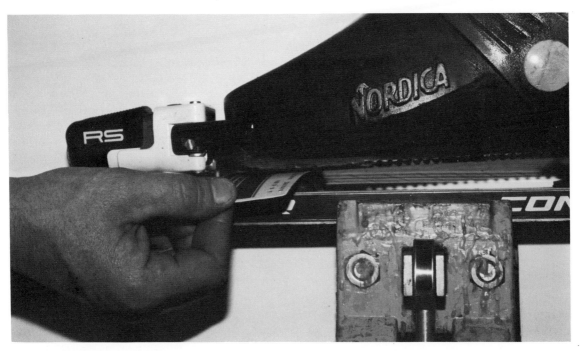

Fig 33   Checking the toe height using a credit card.

Fig 34   Testing the toe tension.

fall unnecessarily. This part of the binding can easily freeze up overnight or even over an extended lunch-break, so it is a good idea to acquire the habit of giving it a quick twist with your hand to ensure that it is working freely before skiing. The heel-piece will free itself by the action of stepping into it.

2. *The heel-piece* To check that this part is correctly adjusted, step into your binding with your boot fastened as it would be if you were skiing. Let's say the ski is on your right leg: step the left foot forward and then vigorously push your right knee towards the tip of the ski; the binding should just release. If it is set too lightly it will pre-release. This manoeuvre may need a couple of attempts before you get it just right, and it might help to have someone standing on the tail of the ski. The heel-piece has a similar window to the toe unit and it is adjusted in the same way, using a screw this time at the rear of the binding.

If your binding bears no relation to my description or if you do not feel confident about making the adjustments, ask the ski-mechanic or your ski-instructor to show you how. They are unlikely to be insured to actually make the adjustments themselves, but they should be able to show you how to make them for yourself.

These tests are by no means foolproof, but in the absence of manufacturer's guidelines they should at least prevent you from skiing on bindings that are too tight for you. If the bindings do come off too easily tighten them up about half a division at a time until they only release in a bad fall. Many very good skiers believe that if you ski properly you can ski on very light settings, but I think that this can be just as dangerous as you then run the considerable risk of them pre-releasing at the slightest error in judgement, resulting in upper limb injuries as bad as a broken leg. Furthermore, some of the techniques in real snow involve considerable rotational forces to be applied to the binding which, if it is set too lightly, will cause it to come off.

(a)

(b)

Fig 35 Testing the heel tension.

Ski Brakes and Leashes

All modern bindings have a ski brake and it is vital that this works correctly; a loose ski quickly picks up speeds of 60 m.p.h. or more and at this speed it could be lethal to someone who has fallen over below you. Unfortunately, as most of you will be aware, ski brakes do not work very well in deep snows. We have all seen the sorry soul digging forlornly in the hope that he will find his ski that has so mysteriously disappeared without trace.

The alternative is to wear powder leashes, but you then run the risk of being hit by the ski in the event of a fall. However, most falls in deep snow, although spectacular because of the explosion of snow, do not normally involve you in the tumbling action that is a real danger with leashes. Another option is to have leashes that are about two metres (2 yards) in length. Store them inside the snow gaiter at the bottom of your ski pants (but these could be even more dangerous). Similar lengths of cord with a floater on the end have been successfully used; the floater rises to the surface making it easier to locate the lost ski.

If you do not want to use leashes and you do lose your ski, the following hints may help you to find it. Mark the spot where you landed with your ski pole and start to search about two to three metres (2 to 3 yards) higher up the slope. It is important that you do not poke around aimlessly: use the tail of your other ski or a partner's ski and slice down the slope at about 25cm (10 inch) intervals. The more you walk over the area, the more likely you are to tread the lost ski deeper into the snow. By being methodical about my searching I have never lost a ski and usually manage to find it quite quickly.

Touring Bindings

It is not quite so easy to deal with touring bindings because they have to perform many different functions and no binding, in my opinion, does them all perfectly. Let us go through these various functions and decide upon some priorities. The first is that, as nearly as possible, the binding should release as well as a downhill model. This presents no problem for the heel unit, but it is quite difficult to include a downhill toe unit. It is my feeling that whichever units are used they should be capable of being released whether the binding is in the uphill or downhill mode. The reason is that people do fall over going uphill and also on short downhill sections where it would take too long to change the mode.

Whether you have to remove the boot in order to alter the mode of the binding is not of great importance, because you always have to take the ski off in order to fix the skins in place. Whatever system is employed to fix the binding in the downhill position, it must allow for the easy removal of any build-up of ice. Also, because of the added friction caused by a Vibram sole, the toe unit must have a compensatory mechanism. The unit should have a climber, which is a simple device allowing the user to climb uphill more easily, and it should be possible to employ this feature without stepping out of the binding. I also find that bindings with a spring-loaded front hinge help with the control of kick turns. Finally, I like systems that allow harschisen (ski crampons) to be fastened either to the ski or to the binding, the reasons for this will be explained in Chapter 7.

Bindings need very little maintenance; all I do is slacken the tension springs at the end of the season. If the internal workings

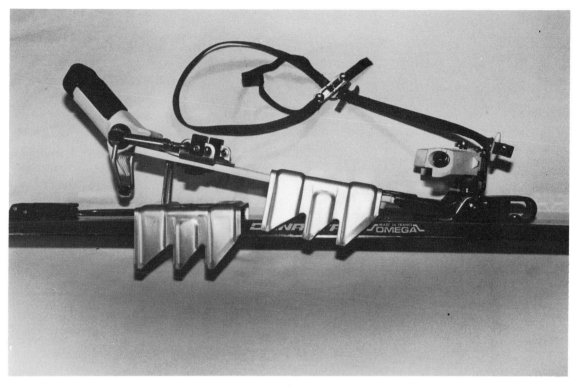

Fig 36 Touring bindings; in the uphill mode. To illustrate the different types I have attached both harschisen instead of just the one you would normally use.

look a little dry, re-grease them. Be sure to use a grease which is recommended by the manufacturer; some greases may not perform correctly at the low temperatures we encounter when skiing.

Poles

Many skiers use poles that are too long. Choose a length according to the criteria illustrated in Fig 37, this will allow for the fact that we ski with our legs bent.

There are two types of hand grip available: the traditional strap and the sword grip. If you use a strap ensure that it is correctly adjusted and preferably of the variety that will release in the event of the pole getting caught. The choice of grip is entirely personal, but if you are touring I would suggest that the strap is more versatile. Paul Rammer, an American who has designed a complete touring system, advocates a grip which incorporates a handle similar to an ice-axe head that can be used to help stop a serious fall. I have never used any of his poles, but have heard some favourable reports.

Some poles have a shaft that can be shortened, but in my experience this is just one more thing to go wrong. They are designed specifically for touring, when carrying the poles on your sack can be awkward. Different length poles can also be useful when climbing on your skis. To overcome the problem of having to hold the poles at half-height I bind a length of string around the shaft for about 20cm

Shovel

The main criteria here are that it should be strong and light, so most of the good ones are made of aluminium and have a curved blade to give added strength. With the advances in modern plastics there are a few shovels that are made of this material, but I have had no experience of them.

The remaining items of equipment are only likely to be used by the ski tourer.

Skins

These are synthetic strips of bristly material that are fixed to the base of the ski and allow the skier to go uphill – they will slide forwards but not backwards. There are numerous systems by which they are fixed to the ski base, the most popular of which is by gluing. The glue remains on the skin and may need replenishing at times. After a while it may form into small globules, and it is then time to remove the old glue and recondition the skin with new glue. The old glue can be removed with a solvent but this is very messy; it is better to use a hot air gun to melt the glue and then scrape it off with a metal scraper. On tour it is wise to carry a small piece of rag with which to wipe away any excess moisture as this will impair the sticking action. The system that I use, and which I have always found very satisfactory, has a small hook on the back of the skin which fastens over the heel of the ski and an elasticated hook for the front.

To store the skins fold the back half on to itself and do the same with the front half, so that all of the sticky surface is covered. The advantage of this method is that when you come to fit the skin you can

Fig 37 Ski poles; choosing the correct length. Notice how the legs are bent. The pole is held upside-down to allow for the tip sinking into the snow.

(8 inches) below the handle. I will explain more about the use of this in Chapter 7. Some touring poles can be screwed together to make an avalanche probe, which, although quite thick and therefore difficult to use, is better than nothing.

There are many different designs of basket. The bigger ones are quite good in the powder, while those which swivel about their centres are best for steep skiing where a stiff basket may make pole planting difficult.

do it one half at a time, thereby preventing snow sticking to the rest of the skin. If the skins get too cold their ability to stick will be affected. Some tourers actually wrap them around their bodies when not in use to keep them warm, but I have always found it sufficient to store them in my sack.

Ice-axe

All you need for touring is a good strong walking axe which will normally be about 60cm (2 feet) in length, anything longer will be unwieldy. There is one type of axe which has a spike that can be extended to form a ski pole, and this might be quite useful if you go in for steep touring. An axe with some form of plastic or rubberised handle is a good choice as it will not feel so cold to handle. It is vital that you keep both the pick and the adze sharp, which can be easily done with a file by simply maintaining the bevels as they exist on the axe already.

Crampons

For ski touring you will generally only need a lightweight pair of ten point cram-

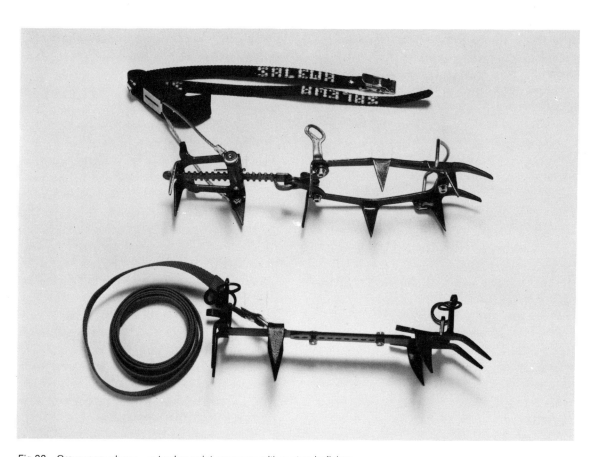

Fig 38   Crampons; above – a twelve point crampon with a step-in fixing;
below – a lightweight touring crampon.

pons, but if you intend using them for any sort of climbing as well you should get the twelve point variety that also have front points. They can be attached to your foot either with straps or with a step-in arrangement similar to some of the old step-in bindings. Whichever system you buy, ensure that it secures the crampon firmly in place and will not fall apart midway through the tour. Again the crampons must be kept sharp if they are to be effective.

Rucksacks

You will need something to carry all this equipment in and the range available is enormous, so here are some criteria to help you to choose. It must be capable of carrying all of your gear and this will mean a capacity of at least 55 litres for most tours, possibly even bigger. I am a great believer that whatever size sack people carry, they will always fill it. I prefer a simple design with few external pockets, but it must have a good hip belt and feel very stable when you are wearing it. On the sides you will need some system by which you can attach the skis. Be wary of some of the purpose-built systems for this function, which I have found to be both weak and the wrong size; simple straps are probably the best.

Rucksacks are not really waterproof, so it is a good idea to pack things in plastic bags. I use small stuff-bags for groups of items, which means that if I want a particular piece of equipment I can get at it easily and without making everything else wet.

3　The Techniques

The main difference between skiing on-piste and in real snow is the variety of snow types that can be experienced. On a pisted run the snow is more or less consistent and any variations that do exist are relatively easy to anticipate. Off-piste, however, the snows can change very subtly, demanding a loose and relaxed style to accommodate these diverse conditions. The constantly changing nature of the snowpack creates another problem, in that no sooner do we begin to master certain conditions than they alter. We all know the frustration of trying to find consistently good powder skiing. For this reason I am going to suggest that you learn a number of techniques first on the piste or even on an artificial slope. It may seem incongruous in a book entitled *Skiing Real Snow* to find the author suggesting you start on an artificial surface, but we have to be practical and make the most of our facilities. If you live close to the snow then, of course, use it, but otherwise use what is available – all time spent on skis will be of benefit.

With this in mind I have structured Chapters 3 and 4 so that you can learn a number of different techniques and then relate them to the snow classification that we adopted in Chapter 1. I am in no doubt that my suggestions as to which techniques are most suited to which snow types will be the centre of many bar-room discussions and will probably raise the eyebrows of many of my fellow ski-instructors. All I ask is that expert and novice alike approach these chapters with open minds and some enthusiasm to experiment.

Learning Techniques

Learning new techniques and improving old ones is all about experimenting. All we, as instructors, can do is to give you guidelines between which you must explore all of the possibilities until you find that which works best for you. Let's take edging the skis as an example. Because of all the variables – the snow, the skis, the variation in body shapes, fitness and strengths – it is impossible to tell you the exact angle to edge the skis; you must learn it through experimentation. I often liken it to learning to drive a car or ride a bike. If you want to stop at the give-way sign at a road junction your instructor will not be able to tell you to depress the brake pedal five centimetres (2 inches) in order to achieve the task. You will succeed at this only after a number of attempts. Many of the techniques in skiing are learned in the same way. Your instructor can give you the parameters within which to work so that you do not waste time and energy on inappropriate movements, but after that it is up to you. Only by varying your movements to the limits of these parameters will you really find out what works best for you and be able to apply the techniques skilfully.

When you watch a good skier floating effortlessly through the powder it is important to remember the miles that the skier has covered in order to reach that stage. Effortless it may appear, but in fact the skier is working hard and is probably also very fit. You cannot hope to improve dramatically with only one week's skiing a year. This was possible when you started, but now that the tasks require a far greater awareness of the medium there are no short-cuts. Imagine playing squash or tennis for only one week a year and expecting vast improvements to take place. The more you want to improve, the harder you will have to work at it, and fortunately even those of us who live many miles from the snows can now get valuable practice on the artificial slopes.

How can I, through the pages of a book, hope to help you when by my own admission miles and miles of skiing is so very important? The first way will be to offer you some of the guidelines, the parameters within which to work. Secondly, you need to understand a little about the way in which we process information so that you can help me to help you. The human brain receives information in a number of different ways, but we need only concern ourselves with three of them: visually, aurally and kinaesthetically. In other words, when you try to interpret the information your instructor gives you, some of you will respond better if they have demonstrated the manoeuvre, others to their verbal description and the rest of you to the sensations that your body received through its other sensory organs.

Good instructors will try to convey their message through all three mediums. They will demonstrate, verbally describe the response wanted and ask for feedback about how certain things felt. You will probably find that one or other of these approaches helps you most. If you respond

best to the demonstration then you are a visualiser; if to the words then your auditory system is the most dominant; and if you perform best by searching for specific sensations in your body then the kinaesthetic strategy is the one to adopt. Before you immediately say you are one or other of these I would like you to test yourself. It is quite hard to establish with certainty which medium suits you best, but try this test. Try to remember a friend's telephone number. As you try to remember it do you picture the sequence, do you say the numbers to yourself, or do you say them with a strong rhythm? If it is the first then your mind adopts a visual strategy to absorb information, the second indicates a dominant auditory system and the last a strong kinaesthetic sense. Establishing the relative role of your kinaesthetic awareness in the learning situation is difficult, but if you are the type of person who has always been quite good at sport and physical things then I would suspect that this is the medium your mind prefers to use to absorb information.

Now, what has all of this to do with reading this book? In order to get the most out of the information contained in these pages you must establish which strategy you learn through and then convert the information into that medium. So if I describe a particular manoeuvre convert it into a sensation, mental picture, or a sequence of key words whichever is appropriate. The text and the diagrams have been specially designed to help you do this.

As you work with the book, I want slowly to encourage your visual and then your kinaesthetic systems to develop. Those rare days when we perform perfectly, our minds seem uncluttered and our skis turn with ease, are probably

Fig 39   Steep skiing in the Himalayas.

occasions on which these systems are functioning more effectively, and we can train ourselves to use them or at least to allow them to operate unhindered.

Visualising

One of the best ways of encouraging the use of these systems is *visualising* (sometimes called imaging). A great many successful athletes from all sports use this technique to enhance their performance. Choose one of the techniques that you want to learn, read the text and look at the accompanying diagrams. The figures in the diagrams are deliberately without faces because I now want you to replace the figure with that of a friend or instructor who you know can perform or is capable of performing this type of turn. In your mind's eye imagine the friend doing these turns, linking one after the other, smoothly and efficiently, just the way you would like to be able to. Run this internal movie a number of times, then replace your friend's face and body with your own and watch yourself performing successfully. Run this movie several times and gradually try to feel your muscles tensing and relaxing through the manoeuvres, feel the cold air on your face, feel the changing pressures on the soles of your feet. Not only are you now seeing yourself performing the turns skilfully, but you are feeling yourself doing them skilfully. Repeat this process the night before you go skiing and then just before you start your run. Be sure to make the mental movie as

Fig 40   A strange sastrugi-like surface on the side of Toubkal, High Atlas Mountains. Turning in one direction was easy, in the other desperate.

realistic as possible: if you are trying the turns on a dry slope picture an artificial slope in your movie, and so on. This type of training needs to be worked at in just the same way as any other technique, but once mastered it should enhance your performance considerably.

Using Your Voice

We can also use our voices effectively in a number of ways. Most of you will have heard the grunts and groans of athletes when they are performing. These noises help to trigger responses from their bodies. Let's take a simple jump as an example. As you perform the movement say the word jump. If you say it softly and weakly your jump will be correspondingly soft and weak; conversely, if your voice is explosive the jump will also be explosive. Our keywords need to be spoken in a manner that invokes the type of response we require.

Once you have overcome the embarrassment of talking aloud to yourself you should find this technique very useful. It also helps with the timing of the manoeuvre and with the timing of your breathing.

Fitness

I spoke earlier of the fitness of the top skiers and how important it is in order to realise your full skiing potential. People are generally more aware of their level of fitness nowadays, and there are many facilities and guidelines available to help you maintain a respectable degree of fitness. I will not expand upon training programmes here because this information is so readily available elsewhere, but I will stress its importance again. If you want to fulfil your potential, embark on a well-structured programme before you intend to go skiing.

Warming Up

One area that I will deal with in more depth is the process of warming up at the start of your day's skiing. I see so many people abusing their bodies in the name of warming up that I am not surprised by the number of injured and sore limbs and muscles that occur. It is very important to warm up on two counts. Firstly, if it is done correctly you will reduce the possibility of injuries and, secondly, it will enable your body to perform well early in the day. The success or failure of the first run often dictates the mood of the day, yet we rarely give that first run a fair chance.

Your warming-up should ideally start in the apartment after breakfast with a stretching programme that covers the whole of your body; this should then be repeated in a shorter form just before your first run. There are basically three different ways to stretch: statically, ballistically, and by a method known as PNF. Ballistically, swinging your limbs about, is the classic way we see people stretching, and it is a very dangerous way, although it is sometimes used by experienced athletes under the guidance of their coach to improve the integrity of the joints. I cannot overemphasise the importance of not stretching in this way, as you will do yourself more harm than good. Each time the muscle you are working on is propelled to the limits of its range of movement (and more than likely beyond it) with this method, you will rupture some of the tissue, and the scar that results will restrict movement in the tissue. A shortening also occurs as a result of the reflex action that the muscle employs to protect itself.

PNF is a system that increases the range of movement by basically working the muscle against a static resistance at the limit of its range of movement and then stretching it. You should only attempt to use this method under supervision, as if it is done incorrectly it could damage the muscles.

That leaves us with static stretching, which is a simple and safe system. You start by stretching until you feel a little tension in the muscle, but very definitely *no* pain. Hold this position for twenty seconds and then stretch a little further until you can feel tension again and hold that position for a further ten seconds, then that's it. I must stress the importance of feeling no pain; if you do, you are tearing the muscle fibres. You should repeat the programme at the end of your day's skiing as this is the best time of all to stretch, and it will help to eliminate much of the soreness that you may have felt on previous trips. Light exercise will also help by removing the waste products that have built up in the muscles during the day – a good excuse to go to the disco!

Once on the slope I do a shortened version of the stretching programme, including some warm-up exercises like running on the spot. This is essential as warming up means just that. I then set off on the first run, taking it carefully, and even using snowploughs for a number of turns just to allow my body to wake up and to feel what the conditions are like. I test my edges by doing fairly edgy turns, but not at any great speed, and I generally try to work my muscles thoroughly. At the end of the run my body is warmed up, but perhaps of even greater significance my mind is confident that my body is performing well and that I am going to ski well that day.

Basic Posture

A good basic posture is fundamental to all forms of skiing, and the first concept to understand is that it is not a static pose. When your body is balanced and your muscles are ready to allow you to move into any position that is necessary to maintain this balance and perform the required manoeuvre, your posture is good. Skiing is a very dynamic sport and your body shape will be continually changing throughout the movements. So what is this position that allows you to perform these incredible feats of athletic prowess? Well, to start with it is not really a position at all, in fact it is largely common sense; you will see what I mean as I explain it.

Before I go any further, however, there is another concept that I would like you to understand. If you are getting down a slope without falling over and hurting yourself, and having a good time as well, then in my opinion you are doing nothing wrong. You may be able to do it better or in a way which will allow you to progress more rapidly, but you are not doing it wrongly. This may seem a minor point, but I believe that this positive attitude helps people to improve more quickly and, furthermore, helps the learning process to become fun, and having fun, surely, is what the whole game of skiing is about.

Feet

Now let's look at this basic posture by starting with the feet. The feet are a major source of feedback about what is happening at one of the most important points –

Fig 41   Good clothing is vital in real snow.

Fig 42   The author before he learned the value of independent leg action. You can almost feel the tensions that were created by this style.

the contact zone between our skis and the snow. Some of you will have been told to stand on your toes, your heels and the whole foot – and all three positions can be valid. To sort out this confusion let's return to our original concept of a neutral posture that is relaxed and balanced. The middle position is obviously one with the pressure over the whole foot; from this position we can move backwards or forwards, we are getting maximum feedback and we are better balanced. Most skiing will, with only one or two exceptions, be done with the pressure spread over the whole foot, although you will not always be aware of this. You may notice that I use the idea of pressure rather than

weight; this is because I think that people are generally much better at relating to where they feel pressure than to where their weight is. The age-old shout of instructors to 'get your weight forwards' usually means *more* forwards. In other words, they are trying to get your weight off the heels and the pressure over the whole foot.

The next point about your feet is one of the most important ideas to grasp in skiing: you must not ski with your feet together. The reason for this is that if you clamp your feet together and then try to rotate them, you will find that you cannot

Fig 43 Alex Leaf - a superb skier of real snow. Notice how the skis offer a
resistance by being edged and how wide apart his feet are, allowing his legs to
act independently. Compare the 'feel' of this photograph to that of Fig 42.

do it without also rotating your hips. This means that your legs are unable to work independently of each other, which in turn severely limits both your balance and your mobility. This is an easy point to prove: stand on a slippery surface in your stockinged feet, clamp them together and turn them. Notice how your hips rotate. Now try to do it quickly and remember how it felt. Repeat the exercise, but this time stand with your feet about hip-width apart. Notice how your hips stay still and also how much quicker you can rotate your legs without things getting out of control. It is also very difficult to edge the downhill ski properly with your feet together.

But all the good skiers ski with their feet together and isn't it necessary to do this in the powder anyway? I hear you argue. Let me answer the former point first. Stand on your slippery surface again, rotate your legs clockwise and now look at your feet. Your left big toe will be touching or nearly touching the heel of your right foot and to an observer it will look as though your feet are together. The gap that you started with now shows itself as a stagger along the length of the foot. When you observe good skiers this is what is happening; it is an illusion that they are skiing with their feet clamped together. I will leave answering the second point until I deal specifically with powder skiing.

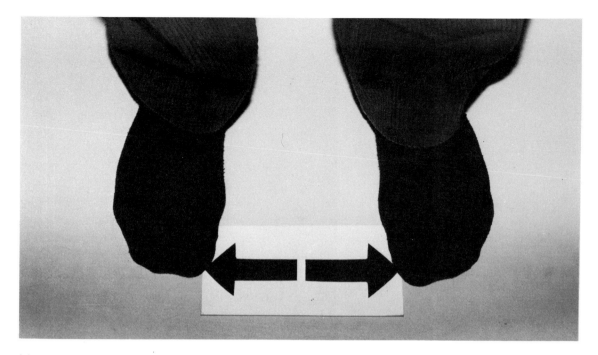

(a)

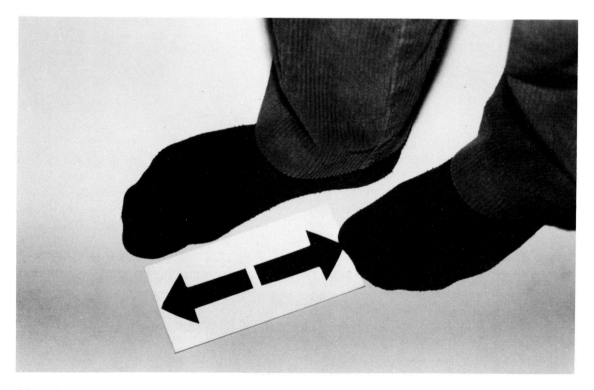

(b)

Fig 44   The illusion that good skiers ski with their feet clamped together.

56

Ankles

I have already discussed the importance of being able to flex your ankles forwards. One of the most frequently quoted sayings of the Continental ski-instructors is 'bend ze knees'; we do exactly that and as a result look as though we are sitting on the lavatory. What I believe they really want us to do is bend our ankles; our knees will then bend naturally and our whole body will feel much more comfortable. You do not need to force your ankles forwards against the boots, just rest them lightly against the tongue. Flexing in this way also enables extension movements to take place and these are essential to many techniques.

Hips

Continuing up the body I will miss out the knees because if your ankles are right your knees will look after themselves. The hips are quite an important region because they affect the upper body, and it is important that this remains as relaxed as possible so that it does not interfere with what the legs are trying to do. Stand upright and then hollow your back; can you feel the tension in your back and shoulders? Now get rid of the hollow and see how this helps to relax the rest of the upper body. By getting rid of the hollowed back we have tilted our pelvis upwards a little, and this position allows a much more dynamic response to any athletic pursuits.

Head, Arms and Hands

The head is held up naturally so that you can see in front of you. You may occasionally want to look at your feet if you are trying a new manoeuvre; don't worry about this to start with as you need the visual feedback. However, at your standard, after a couple of runs you should be looking ahead again.

The factors that influence the position of your arms and hands are that they assist with your balance and pole planting. Climb up on to a chair, jump off and land as softly as possible; notice the position of your arms. Alternatively, balance along a narrow beam in a gym or on a kerb stone. In both these cases, most of you will notice that you are holding your arms out to the side and slightly in front of you (a little high, perhaps, in the case of the jump). One of the best ways of describing this position is to imagine you are holding a hoop around your hips. If twelve o'clock is directly in front of you, position your hands at ten o'clock and at two o'clock. This position should roughly correspond to the one you found yourself in earlier. Not only is it good for balance, but when you plant your poles you can do so with very little arm movement and in such a way that the forces transmitted by the pole plant will pass up to the upper body via the bones and not stress any of the ligaments or tendons.

Most people have a part of their body which, if they can relax it, helps them to relax the rest of their body. When I am driving my car I often find myself gripping the steering wheel quite tightly, this in turn tenses my shoulders and neck and consequently makes me tired. If I relax my thumbs it seems to act as a trigger and relaxes the rest of my shoulder girdle. When I am skiing the key lies in relaxing my shoulders; having discovered this I now always give them a quick shrug as I set off down a run. Finding your key can only be done by trial and error and listening to your body.

Fig 45   Skiing in the trees. This is the place to head for if the visibility is poor.

Fig 46   Skiing a steep gulley. Notice how the skier has taken off on his uphill ski.

Fig 47   Skinning in the High Atlas Mountains.

This, then, is our basic posture. Remember, it is not a rigidly held position, but one from which we can move dynamically and return to if in need of balance. It is essential to be aware of it in order to make optimum progress. We will now look at each technique in turn.

1,000 Step Turn

This is really our first survival turn (that is, if we disregard traversing and kick turning which will be dealt with later), but it is also a very useful exercise.

Choose a fairly shallow slope and traverse it. When you reach the other side, simply step uphill making small steps with your edges until you stop. Now try the same thing in the other direction. Still maintaining a shallow traverse, repeat the exercise but this time continue walking around in a full circle until you are facing in the other direction. The ability to walk your skis around in this way is very important, yet it is often neglected. To be able to lift your skis and place them in a new direction is the most basic way of changing course.

Having successfully completed the above manoeuvre try the same exercise from a steeper traverse, but miss out the 360 degree turn and instead step down the slope and start a new turn. Ultimately you are aiming to link a number of turns together, stepping continuously throughout. If you are experiencing difficulty with this manoeuvre, first try it on a shallower slope with very small but continuous steps; then, when you can confidently 'run' all over it, move on to a steeper slope.

Finally, there are three ways in which we can lift the ski: we can lift its tail, its front, or the whole ski. Practise all of them as they all have their uses.

Stem Turns

These turns cover a host of different types, and although I want to keep everything as simple as possible I do feel it is important to clarify some points so that you do not get confused by the different ski schools' ideas.

Those of you who learned many years ago will probably remember the trauma of trying to get rid of the stem in your turns. One of the reasons was that you were probably taught to spread your legs out into a stem at the start of the turn and then to bring them together again to finish in a christie (swing to the hill). This adduction and abduction of the legs does not occur in the parallel turn, so when you tried to make the transition this action, which by now was probably a habit, interfered with the new movements needed. A better way into ploughing (for the person trying to learn parallels) is to do it with a rotational movement of the leg. This will not interfere as parallel turns contain this same element. This technique forms part of the basic swing method which is a progression of turns leading to parallels. It is important for the learner not to confuse this with the stem turn that I am about to describe, otherwise it may hinder their progress.

The stem turn is a very versatile off-piste turn and was one of the first turns ever to be described. It has several forms, so I will break it down into its essential elements. Again, choose a fairly shallow slope and set off on a traverse. If the snow is inconsistent, check it by stemming the downhill ski and feeling with this foot until it feels stable enough to turn, at this

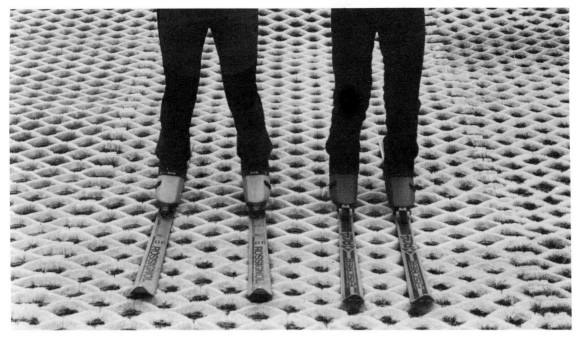

(a)

(b)

Fig 48   The skier on the right is abducting the leg in order to reach the plough position (the legs move away from the mid-line of the body), whereas the skier on the left is rotating the leg (a small amount of abduction has occurred but it is minimal).

The stem turn (basic)

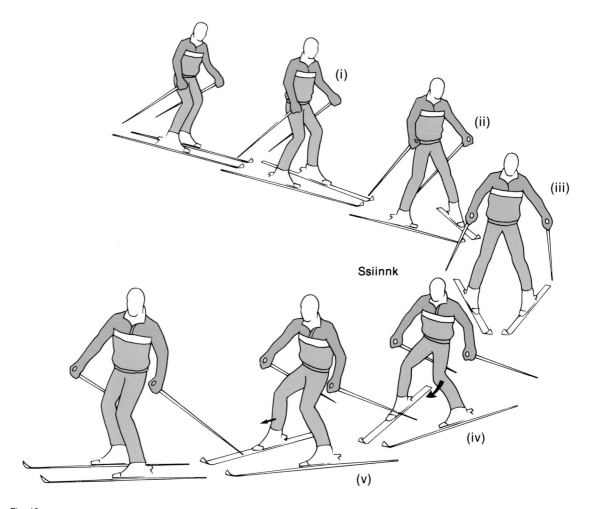

Fig 49

(i) Check the snow conditions with the pole and the downhill ski. When it feels good stem the uphill ski (if this is awkward stem both and do not be in a hurry, let the skis flow into the new position).

(ii) Reach the plough position by either pushing the skis into place with no up-motion of the legs or by standing up high which will help if you want to sink powerfully later.

(iii) Allow the skis to flow downhill. Some acceleration will be felt; in poor conditions a wider plough will reduce this acceleration.

(iv) Powerfully steer the downhill ski around the turn, driving the knee forwards and in. A sinking action over this ski will help. Concentrate solely on the downhill ski, balancing firmly over it. Use the word *sink*, powerfully drawing the word out as long as is necessary.

(v) A pole plant may be useful to give extra support as you return the uphill ski to the **traverse position. Pushing this ski forwards** will help you to achieve this.

The swing to the hill

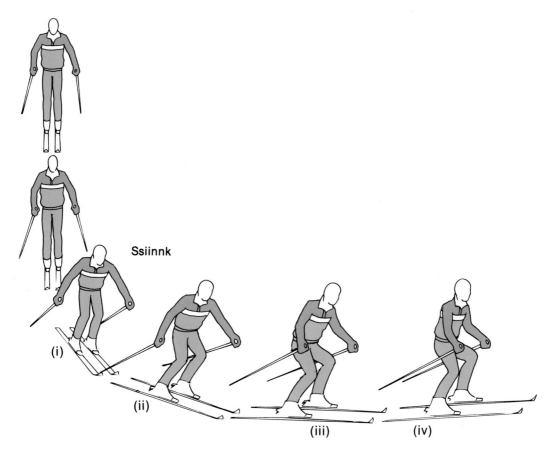

Ssiinnk

(i)

(ii)

(iii)

(iv)

Fig 50

(i) Sink down over the downhill ski, using the word *sink* as you do so. Concentrate only on the downhill ski, but if this does not have the desired effect try lifting the uphill ski very slightly.

(ii) Drop your hip to the inside of the turn (the amount will depend upon how fast you are going; more speed more drop). Make sure the uphill ski is in front of the downhill ski. Feel the pressure along the inside of the downhill foot.

(iii) Check that all of the parallel lines are still parallel. Feel the pressure building up against your shin bone and grade it; (0 (nothing) – 5 (painful). Call out the grade throughout the turn, making it higher towards the end of the turn.

(iv) Practise varying the position of the pressure under your feet and against your shin bone.

point stem both skis. If conditions are easy it is more normal to stem only the uphill ski. This stemming action can be done with a leg extension which then allows you to drop into the swing, or it can be done from a mid-stance posture with minimal flexing and extending of the legs.

Whichever system you have used, as you pressurise the uphill ski your skis will start to flow downhill. The point at which you bring them together and finish the turn with what is known as a swing to the hill will vary with conditions. At this stage you should practise bringing them together almost immediately and, at the other extreme, practise holding the plough all the way through the turn until you can return to the traverse. The pole plant can be used at this moment to give you added security.

Practise your swing to the hill so that you can do it both subtly and aggressively. To do it aggressively use your knees by driving them forwards and into the slope. I can usually feel a lot of pressure against my shin bones and the skis are edged so that I can feel my big toe of the downhill ski pressing hard against the boot sole. You can also use your hips by dropping them into the turn, but this is only suitable if you are going fairly fast. I often imagine that there is a big pile of loose snow in front of me, and so that it will not knock me over I power my knees forwards to force the skis through the obstacle.

Having accomplished the manoeuvre in this aggressive manner, now try it in a number of other ways. First, pay attention to the pressures under your feet and try to achieve the swing with the pressure evenly distributed along the sole of your foot and then with it on the heel of your foot. All are possible with practice and all have a value under certain circumstances. Prac-

tise the swing with a strong sinking action and then with very little extension or retraction. The importance of the swing to the hill cannot be overemphasised, as not only is it the second half of a parallel turn but it also sets you up for the next turn.

If you are experiencing problems with your swings to the hill, check that your uphill ski is in front of the downhill ski – this ensures that your body is balanced over the downhill ski. Try to manoeuvre lifting the tail of the uphill ski throughout or advancing it at the start, and get a friend to check that your ski tips, feet, knees, hips, shoulders and arms are all in parallel lines to each other. The problem will probably be connected to the misalignment of one of these.

The stem turn in all its various guises should be practised, because it can be used in a variety of different situations and can be a real life-saver in some conditions.

Jump Turns

These are another very basic form of turning, which are also quite versatile. First, you should practise the jump by choosing a shallow traverse and, whilst traversing, hop the heels of your skis off the ground by extending the legs strongly at the moment you plant your downhill pole. The pole is acting as a trigger. You should feel as though your heels are trying to come out of the boots. Soften the landing by allowing your legs and ankles to flex; this will also prepare you for the next jump. Once you feel happy with these, try to initiate your parallel turns with the same movement.

Start by flowing down the slope, swing to the hill and, as your edges grip and you feel the resistance building up at the end of

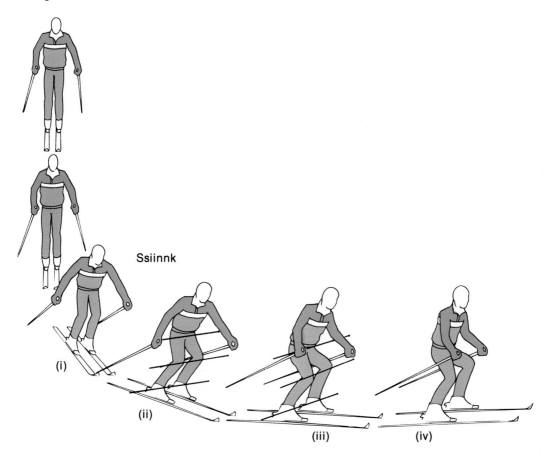

Ssiinnk

(i)

(ii)

(iii)

(iv)

Fig 51   Maintaining the parallel lines in a swing to the hill.

the swing, plant the pole, jump the skis into the flow-line again and repeat in the other direction. Continue down the slope, concentrating on the rhythm of the turns. Rhythm is an extremely important element of off-piste skiing, and I will be continually emphasising it throughout these chapters. You can use the pole plant to help with the initiation of the turn; the moment the pole is planted it acts like a trigger to signal the start of the jump. It only needs to touch the snow lightly and is really only an aid to time the turns.

The concept of a flow-line as opposed to the fall-line may help you. Whatever turns you do, you will probably feel moments when you are resisting and moments when you are flowing. Try to feel this in some simple turns: flow then resist, flow then resist - enjoy these contrasting sensations. I have always felt that a significant breakthrough occurs when a skier enjoys the acceleration that usually accompanies the flow. The flow-line will often, but not necessarily, be close to the fall-line. However, the fall-line is really unimportant, whereas an appreciation of the point at which you begin to flow and then resist will help your turns to feel smoother and more rhythmical.

The stem turn (advanced; a stem christie)

(i) Stem the uphill ski with an accompanying up-motion.

(ii) Pole plant and move the downhill ski parallel to the uphill ski, this will allow you to drop your hip into the turn.

(iii) Swing to the hill projecting your skis around the curve of the turn.

Fig 52

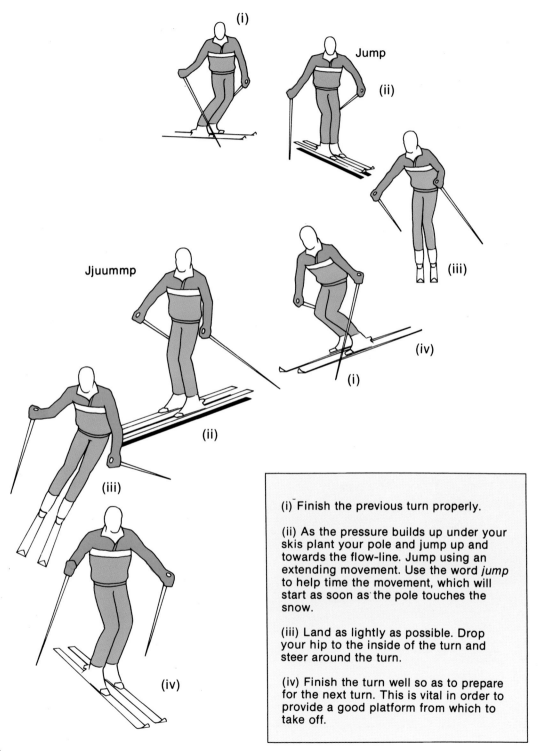

(i) Finish the previous turn properly.

(ii) As the pressure builds up under your skis plant your pole and jump up and towards the flow-line. Jump using an extending movement. Use the word *jump* to help time the movement, which will start as soon as the pole touches the snow.

(iii) Land as lightly as possible. Drop your hip to the inside of the turn and steer around the turn.

(iv) Finish the turn well so as to prepare for the next turn. This is vital in order to provide a good platform from which to take off.

Fig 53

If you find it difficult to jump the skis, concentrate on the swing phase. In other words, it is the finish of the previous turn that is causing the problem because it is not providing a platform from which you can jump. Exaggerate all your actions; imagine you are the instructor and, like all good instructors, you want to show your pupils exactly what to do, so emphasise these movements. Call them out as you go – *jjjuuummmppp* – feel the word reaching up into the air like your body, float there for a moment and then sink down softly.

These turns are very simple, but nevertheless effective and useful in many situations.

Short Swings

These turns are often used by skiers to develop their co-ordination and rhythm, but for the skier of real snow they can be very useful in steep narrow gulleys. There are a number of variations which depend upon the way you jump and the point about which your skis pivot. It is possible to jump in two different ways. I described one, using a strong leg extension, earlier. The other is achieved by pulling the legs up sharply below you; this is known as a leg retraction. Try them both, one after the other, you will notice that the leg extension is a slower type of jump than the leg retraction, which is a very rapid movement.

Leg Extension

Let's look at the leg extension short swings first, as they are really only a progression from the simple jump turns that we have already used. One of the most important points is the concept of the platform that is needed in order to jump cleanly. If the skis are skidding, it is very difficult to jump so we have to create a platform. This is achieved by driving the knees powerfully forwards and into the slope during the swing phase of the turn, especially just before the commencement of the next turn. The pressure at this moment should be felt on your heels, not so much that you are actually leaning against the back of the boots but still very definitely on the heels. Then, as you jump, the pressure will move forwards to the ball of your foot and to the instep. This movement is known as a *check*, and if you examine your tracks carefully after performing one of these turns you

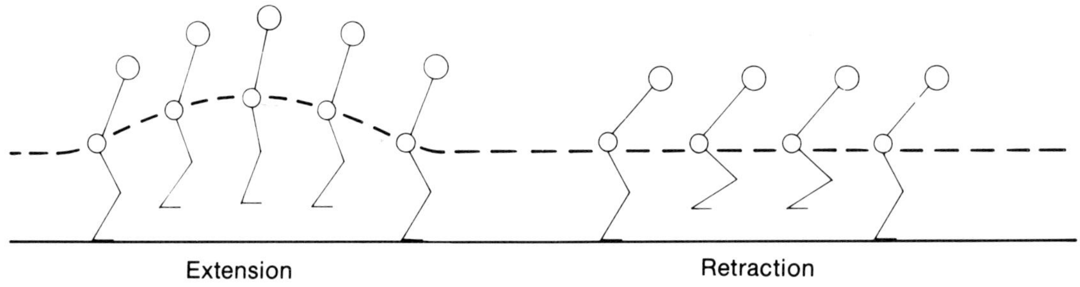

Extension   Retraction

Fig 54   Extension and retraction.

Short swings with leg extension

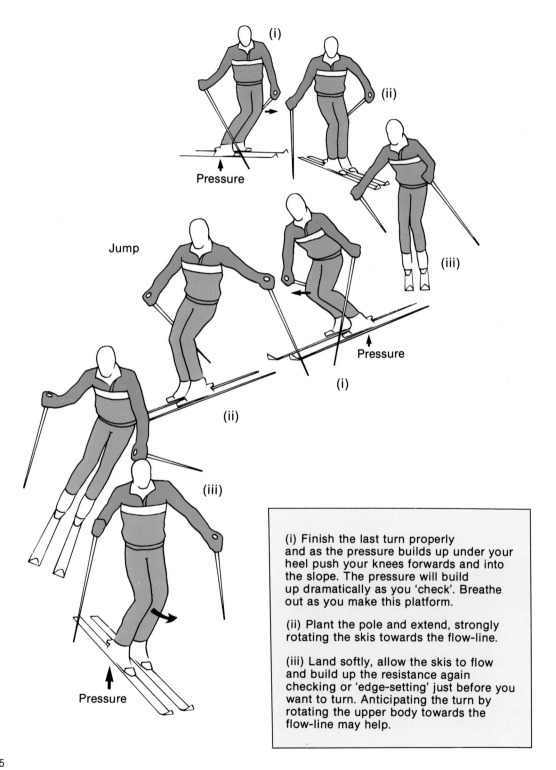

Pressure

Jump

Pressure

(i)

(ii)

(iii)

(i)

(ii)

(iii)

Pressure

(i) Finish the last turn properly
and as the pressure builds up under your
heel push your knees forwards and into
the slope. The pressure will build
up dramatically as you 'check'. Breathe
out as you make this platform.

(ii) Plant the pole and extend, strongly
rotating the skis towards the flow-line.

(iii) Land softly, allow the skis to flow
and build up the resistance again
checking or 'edge-setting' just before you
want to turn. Anticipating the turn by
rotating the upper body towards the
flow-line may help.

Fig 55

will see the platform that has been created by this action in the snow. At this point the skis are often at nearly 90 degrees to the flow-line, so you will have to jump quite hard to return to a position from which you can flow.

A good way of learning these turns, which rely heavily on rhythm for success, is to choose a long, smooth, but fairly steep slope and to start off by doing simple long radius jump turns. Gradually narrow the radius of the turns, increase their frequency and at the same time start to exaggerate all of the movements. Imagine you are skiing down an ever narrowing funnel, so that the turns become quicker and quicker and also tighter and tighter. The secret is to tighten the turns very gradually and to really exaggerate the movements. Without thinking about it you will probably have been turning your skis about a point some 10 to 20 centimetres (4 to 8 inches) back from the tips of the skis. I find this the most natural point to rotate the skis about when I use leg extension type jumps, but you should also try to move the point of rotation back first to your feet and then even to the tails, although this last is quite tricky. Versatility is the name of the game, however.

Leg Retraction

Leg retraction short swings are probably best done with the pivot point about the middle of the ski, allowing the skis to be turned quickly in a very small space. To learn this type of turn, choose a slope of medium steepness which is not too long and has an easy run-out at the bottom. The snow should, ideally, be soft enough for the edges to bite easily and you should not feel fearful of the slope. Start in a fairly wide stance; this is essential so that the

legs can be freely rotated, leaving the body facing down the flow-line. Now jump down the slope, rotating the skis each time and landing firmly on the new edges (in some conditions it may be desirable to let the skis skid a little to kill some of the speed). As you land, reach down the slope for your next pole plant. This action will achieve two things: it will help to stabilise your landing by adding a third point of support, and it will also make you angulate correctly, allowing the edges to bite better.

Personally I do not believe it is worth refining this turn into a super-smooth, softer type of turn, because when we use it in real situations in steep narrow gulleys it is best done in its simplest form just as it is described above. This is not to say you should not practise; just keep them simple. Indeed, improving them so that you can perform the turns very quickly and precisely is an excellent exercise.

Rhythm

With all short swings rhythm is vitally important, and to help with this you can again use your voice effectively. Every time you plant the pole shout *jump* and on landing *siiinnnk*, the length of the word being dependent upon the type of turn you want. This use of words will also help with your breathing which must be kept in time with your actions. After a while, you will probably be able to dispense with the words and just concentrate on your breathing. Inhale with the jump and exhale as you land and control the swing phase.

I have seen short swings taught in a hundred different ways; all of them are probably valid as exercises, but many of them would be unsuitable if we were to try to use them in real situations where we are forced by the terrain to ski the fall-line but

Short swings and leg retraction

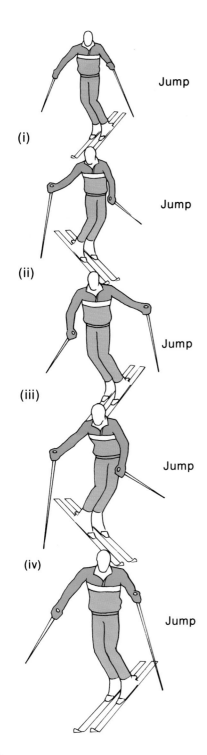

Jump

(i)

Jump

(ii)

Jump

(iii)

Jump

(iv)

Jump

Fig 56

(i) Legs apart.

(ii) Plant the pole wide so as not to block your body. Pivot the skis about your feet, the amount will depend upon the steepness of the slope.

(iii) Land on the new edges, skidding if necessary. I find breathing out forcibly at this moment helps.

(iv) Rhythm is vital; try to maintain it even though some of the turns do not feel right. Using an audible signal and breathing properly will help, as will planting the pole and using it as a timing device.

do not want to pick up much speed, and cannot do it by using long turns. Obviously these criteria will vary from skier to skier, but I think these situations are fairly rare for most of us, and the leg extension turns are the most likely ones to be of use unless you aspire to be a skier of the steep.

Compression Turns

These turns are one of the most useful techniques for skiing real snow. The best way to learn them is to find some small bumps (moguls) and practise absorbing them. Choose a slow traverse angle and imagine you are carrying a tray of very valuable cut-crystal glasses. To prevent them falling over you must keep the tray level, and you can do this by allowing your legs to bend and stretch through the crests and hollows. At first this is a passive action: as your skis hit the bump you allow your knees to rise up towards your chest until the top is reached and then you extend your legs into the next trough keeping the skis in contact with the snow throughout. As you go faster, so the action

71

becomes more and more active with you positively pulling your legs up and pushing them down.

Now try a turn: find a small bump and approach it as before, but this time when you reach the crest rotate the skis into the new direction before extending your legs again. This action will be helped by planting the pole slightly on the downhill side of the bump. Planting the pole late in this way will help to delay the moment you try to turn your legs. It is common for people to turn too early when they first try these turns. One of the advantages of this turn is that it is possible to do parallel turns very slowly whereas all other parallel turns need to be done at speed. Also, because of the extra rotational leverage your thighs have when the knees are bent at 90 degrees, it is a very powerful way of turning.

These turns require practice, because the leg movement may be quite different to what you are accustomed to doing. Many of you will find that it takes a while to stop standing up on top of the bump. If this is the case, try doing the turn very slowly, making sure your head stays level with your pole planting hand at the crest of the mogul. Alternatively try to visualise someone in front of you and freeze-frame

them at the crest; feel the tension in your thighs, notice the position of your hands and sense the tightness of your stomach muscles. It may be necessary to feel only one of these sensations, but visualise it several times and then do the manoeuvre.

Another way would be to use your voice: as you approach the mogul say to yourself *ffooollldddd*. As you go faster, sharpen the word up and say it louder as the action becomes more explosive *FFOLLD!* This will not only remind you of the required action, but will help both with the timing and your breathing.

(i) Pole plant a fraction after the bump. Absorb the bump.

(ii) *Fold* – use your voice again. Feel the tension in your thighs and stomach muscles. Head level with your hand. Anticipate the turn by rotating your body to face towards the new direction.

(iii) Extend your legs into the hollow so that your body remains level. Imagine you are holding a tray of cut-crystal glasses.

(iv) Extend the legs fully, keeping the skis in contact with the snow.

(v) The pole is beginning to reach forwards for the next pole plant.

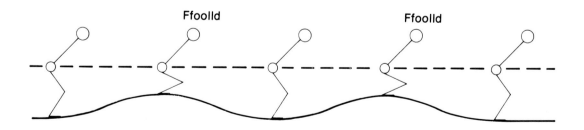

Ffoolld   Ffoolld

Fig 57 Absorbing bumps. The head and hips stay level and the legs flex in order to absorb the terrain.

Compression turns

(i)

Ffoolld

(ii)

(iii)

(iv)

(v)

Fig 58

Having gained some degree of success on these small bumps I now want to move you back on to the piste. Remember, we are learning these turns for use in real snow not for mogul bashing. This is not to decry the pleasure of skiing the bumps, but it is not the intention of this book to cover those techniques. Choose a wide green run and set off, flow down and do a swing to the hill. At the end of the swing stay low and turn the skis until they flow again, extending your legs to resist, bending them again to flow and so on down the slope. Your body may rise and fall through the turn but the pressure under your feet should remain fairly consistent throughout. A good exercise for these turns is to hold the poles at half-height and, keeping your body in a position that enables you to plant the poles easily, perform a number of linked turns. With practice you will be able to lower your grip even further.

Hip Rolling Turns

Two types of turn which use this compression idea, albeit more subtly, are what I will call simply knee rolling and hip rolling turns. Again choose a large wide green run and start to schuss down the middle. Adopt a slightly lower posture than normal (but not as low as in the previous exercise). When you are going quite fast drop your right hip to the right, and then as you turn move your hips over to the left, keeping them level as you do so. Repeat this with a steady tempo and after several turns you should find a really relaxed rhythm establishing itself. You should feel as though you are rolling your hips from one side to the other, and that is all you are doing to initiate the turns. (I am, of course, assuming that the rest of your basic technique is good.) If the turns do not feel easy, try dropping your hips even further into them and maybe moving from one turn to the next sooner. If you are keeping your hips level you will find that the pressure under your feet remains almost constant throughout the turns as before.

These are good turns to experiment with a technique known as foot thrusting. As you start the new turn, thrust your feet forwards through the turn; it should feel as if you are accelerating your skis around the curve. The pressure will start on the heels, move to the middle and then to the balls of the feet. To complete the turn move the feet forwards to feel the pressure in the middle again and so on. This is actually a very useful technique; once you have felt it in these turns try to introduce it to the other compression turns.

Knee Rolling Turns

A variation on these hip rolling turns are knee rolling turns. Return to the same wide green piste and adopt a similar posture, but with your feet slightly wider apart than normal. Start down the flowline and roll your knees from side to side. The first few turns, as always, will feel cumbersome, but as you let the rhythm take over so the turns begin to take care of themselves, your legs feel as if they are made of rubber and the skis almost turn of their own accord. The result is a fast, flowing, edgy type of turn, which makes you feel that you are using the skis to their maximum advantage.

A word of warning is necessary, however; these turns can stress your knees to a considerable degree, so do not attempt them unless you are very fit and regularly ski fast and hard.

Hip rolling turns with foot thrusting

(i) Roll your hips to the inside of the turn thrusting your feet forwards at the same time.

(ii) As the turn comes to an end prepare to roll your hips to the other side.

Roll

(i)

Roll

(ii)

Fig 59

Surf Turns

A further development of the compression turn (or as the French call it *avalement*) is what Joubert, one of the world's most innovative ski teachers, calls the surf turn. Joubert noticed that many of the best racers and off-piste skiers were occasionally adopting a stance that allowed them either to glide or edge the ski with great precision and furthermore to change from one to the other very quickly. As he began to analyse this movement and teach it to his students at Grenoble University, he gave it the name of surf technique because of its similarity to the stance that surfers and skateboarders use.

It is a dynamic posture in that it is constantly changing throughout the turn, but we can understand some of the elements without actually skiing. Take a couple of chairs and, using them to support yourself, put both feet over to one side then flatten your feet. You should find that your knees are bent at about 90 degrees, and that in order to flatten your feet your ankles will also have to be at this angle. This is the surf posture; it is similar to the one you used in the compression turn except that you have much greater control over your edges. It is a strenuous style and you need to be both skiing well

Fig 60   A skier practising compression turns on a dry slope; make the most of what you have!

Fig 61 A skateboarder using the 'surf stance'. Notice how the knees are tending to be pushed to the outside of the turn.

on a monoski. If you ski the troughs of a mogul slope with no braking, you will begin to feel this new action with your knees displaced to the outside of the turn. The pressure under your feet remains the same throughout, and if you can maintain the speed it feels very smooth. Similarly, on a monoski in the bumps you will find yourself skiing in this new style, and in deep heavy snow it is almost a natural action to allow the feet to flatten, thus flattening the skis, otherwise the turns will be too tight. I will expand on this idea in Chapter 4.

Once you have felt this new action try it in some of the other turns I have described; in some it will feel good, in others a little contrived. It is not a technique to be used exclusively; variety, to repeat myself, is the name of the game.

Foot Lifting

This type of turn is very useful when you need to be on your edges throughout the turn, for example when you are skiing ice. Choose a nice wide green or blue run, perhaps a little steeper than those you used before because you need to be going a little faster. Head off on a steep traverse line to your left as you face down the slope. When you have picked up a reasonable amount of speed, lift the heel of your right ski by retracting your right leg and *think* about turning to a point on the other side of the piste. In other words, do not try to analyse what you are doing, because by the time you have, it will be too late. All that is necessary is to think about being at this new point; your body will react appropriately to the rest. This may sound vague to many of you so I will explain a little about what is happening to give you the

and fit before you attempt it.

Try the hip rolling turns with foot thrusting, and as your skis reach the outermost part of the turn try to flatten them by allowing your ankles to roll and your knees to push to the outside of the turn. Joubert, in fact, suggested that you first try these turns in very difficult snows as they are one of the few turns that will work and you will therefore feel their value immediately.

Two other occasions when I have felt the surf action have been in the bumps and

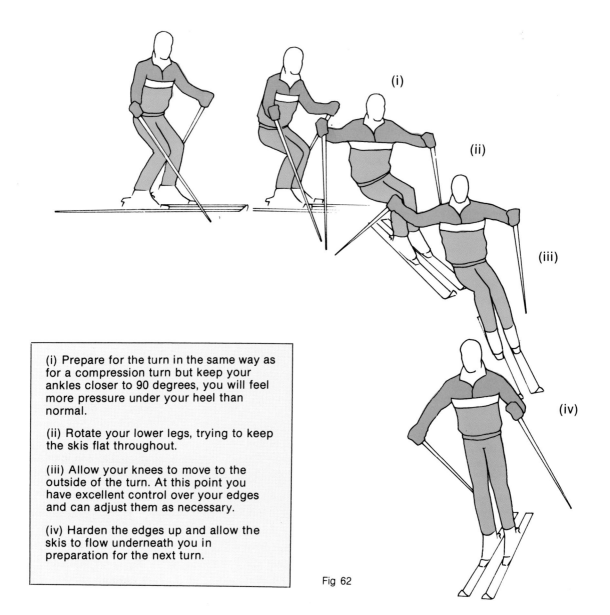

(i) Prepare for the turn in the same way as for a compression turn but keep your ankles closer to 90 degrees, you will feel more pressure under your heel than normal.

(ii) Rotate your lower legs, trying to keep the skis flat throughout.

(iii) Allow your knees to move to the outside of the turn. At this point you have excellent control over your edges and can adjust them as necessary.

(iv) Harden the edges up and allow the skis to flow underneath you in preparation for the next turn.

Fig 62

confidence to try it.

When you are traversing, gravity is trying to pull you straight down the hill (this is not strictly true, but is close enough). Your skis are biting and preventing this from happening so you go across

instead. If you remove the ski that is biting or resisting the pull of gravity, your hips will drop into the new turn and you will start to travel downhill, which is also in the direction of the next turn. (My apologies to the physicists amongst you, but I

Foot lifting turns

Lift and sink

(i)

(ii)

(iii)

(i) You must be going fast. Retract the downhill leg. Do not straighten the uphill leg, but rather bend it down further at the same time as lifting the other one. *Lift* and *sink*.

(ii) Think about getting to the new position, the point to which you want the turn to take you.

(iii) Shuffle forwards the foot you have lifted.

Fig 63

want to keep it as simple as possible because I don't believe that understanding the mechanics of the turn will help you turn any easier, in fact quite the contrary.) So, by removing the downhill ski you allow yourself to flow, with the help of gravity, smoothly into the next turn. Once you have initiated the turn you can rest the lifted ski back on to the ground, but do not put any pressure on to it. Initiating the turn in this way ensures that you are pressurising the new ski right at the beginning of the turn and also that you will be on the new edge very early on in the turn, both of which are important factors in skiing ice or hardpack.

There are several different ways in which you can remove the resisting ski: you can lift the heel, the whole foot, the front of the ski or, very subtly, simply slide the ski forwards. Lifting the heel maintains a good low balanced position, but does not emphasise the importance of sliding the foot forwards which will keep it depressurised. Lifting the tip of the ski does, and some ski teachers prefer this approach. I prefer lifting the heel and then shuffling the foot forwards as this is not quite such a dynamic turn as the former,

and as such more people seem able to cope with it. Try both and see which works best for you. Another bonus of lifting the tip is that it encourages you to carve off the tail of the ski. Just sliding the ski forwards is a very relaxing way of initiating turns and as an action can be incorporated into most parallel turns.

If you are experiencing problems it will probably be because you are not removing the resisting ski at the very start of the turn. Use your voice again to aid with the timing by shouting *lift* at the precise moment you want to start turning. Add the words *and shuffle* if the depressurised ski is not in front of the other ski. Make sure you lift the ski with a retraction; if you straighten the other leg you will counteract some of the important elements. It is useful sometimes to lift and sink as this helps the hip to drop into the new turn. Another common error is not going fast enough; the turn relies on a reasonable amount of speed. Finally, you must believe that after lifting the ski you will turn to your new objective; look for the new point and go for it. Once mastered I doubt that you will want to turn by any other method again, these feel so easy!

THE GAMES

In the first section we looked at the techniques and knowledge which are necessary to move into the world of off-piste skiing in relative safety and which will help us to enjoy this exciting game. I have called it a game on purpose, not to devalue it but to put it into perspective. It is important to remember that off-piste skiing can be enjoyed at many different levels and in a number of different ways. You do not have to be able to ski the powder with absolute precision to enjoy it; you can have fun skiing it with stem turns or even just schussing straight down easy-angled slopes, feeling the ice-cold spray billowing up around you. Many a mountaineer who, with little skiing ability, has taken to ski touring can testify to this notion.

In the second section I will describe the games that are possible and give you some ideas about how best to enjoy them. This is where the fun really begins!

4 Skiing Real Snow

The time has now come to relate the techniques to the variety of different snow conditions that we experience off-piste. The table lists these conditions and summarises which techniques are most appropriate to various situations. It is by no means exclusive, and the very best off-piste skiers can ski different snow types in any number of ways, but it forms a good basis from which to experiment.

Technique / Snow type	Stem turns	Step turns	Jump turns	Short swings Front	Mid	Back	Compression turns	Surf turns	Hip rolling	Knee rolling	Foot lifting
Light shallow	*		*				*	*	*	*	
Light deep	*						*	*	*	*	
Bottomless powder							*	*			
Heavy shallow	*	*	*		*		*	*	*		
Heavy deep	*		*			* steep	*	*			
Crust consistent	*	*	*		*		*				*
Crust variable	*	*					*	*			
Spring snow	*	*	*	*	*		*	*	*	*	
Mixed terrain	*						*	*			
Ice & hardpack											*
The steep					*						
Bad visibility	*		*	*			*				

Light and Shallow

These are perfect conditions in which to start your real snow career. You can ski just as though you were on piste; the snow usually has a beautifully creamy texture and your skiing should feel very smooth. Concentrate on smooth actions and do not look at your skis, they will take care of themselves providing you ski normally. Do not be tempted to lean back; feel the pressure over the middle of your foot. I will expand upon the idea of leaning back in the following section on light and deep conditions.

Light and Deep

This is the most common type of powder. It can be very deep but will have a base to it and can be skied in a variety of ways.

There are a number of misconceptions about skiing powder, most of which originated many years ago when equipment was very different. The first is that you should sit back or lean back in the powder so that your ski tips float to the surface and do not dive. Years ago when skis were generally much stiffer this may well have been necessary, but with modern softer skis it is not. You can ski the powder this way but it is unnecessarily tiring. The modern ski does not have to be physically brought to the surface before you start the next turn unless the snow is heavy or unless you are skiing very slowly, which even the most timid of skiers will rarely be doing. When you watch someone skiing the powder it will often look as though their weight is back, but that is usually an illusion because you are not taking into account the angle of the slope and the snow.

Another misconception is that you must keep your skis flat. This method can indeed be used, but most people actually find it easier to over edge the skis when they are learning to ski these conditions. You never feel the edges biting as such, but the action of trying to make them bite will help the ski to turn. It is desirable, however, to keep the pressure on your feet fairly evenly distributed, but not by clamping your feet together. If you pressurise your feet in the normal way you will find that one ski will tend to float to the surface before the other. This makes them difficult to control, although I have seen some very good racers ski the powder like this. In a way this sums up powder skiing, in that it is possible to ski it in any number of different ways. However, we will now look at some of the easier methods.

Methods

Let's assume that this is your first attempt at skiing the deep; you have skied the light and shallow snow and now you feel ready to emulate the stars of all those amazing ski films. Find a pleasant shallow slope which you will feel happy schussing and start by just schussing it. As you descend, alter your balance so you feel the pressure on your toes, the middle of your feet and then on your heels. Move your balance as far forwards as you can without allowing the skis to bury themselves and then try to relax in this position. Do some of the schussing exercises you learned as a beginner, particularly those involving the upper body, such as passing your poles around your body or swinging your arms from side to side without it affecting your lower body. Your aim is to be able to schuss in a posture that enables you to relax the upper body totally.

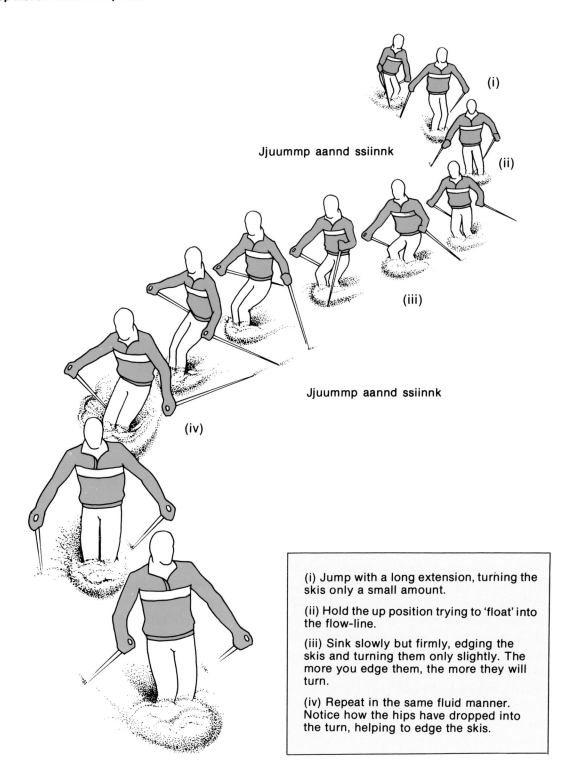

Jjuummp aannd ssiinnk

(i)

(ii)

(iii)

Jjuummp aannd ssiinnk

(iv)

(i) Jump with a long extension, turning the skis only a small amount.

(ii) Hold the up position trying to 'float' into the flow-line.

(iii) Sink slowly but firmly, edging the skis and turning them only slightly. The more you edge them, the more they will turn.

(iv) Repeat in the same fluid manner. Notice how the hips have dropped into the turn, helping to edge the skis.

Fig 64

Fig 65   A beautiful glade. The skier has removed his hands from the pole straps to prevent injury if the poles get caught in a branch.

On the next run continue to schuss, but this time jump up and down in slow motion; like a ball bouncing you should never stay in one position – there should be constant motion. It is important that you try to do this exercise in slow motion, because if your actions are too quick you will soon lose control. Use the visualising technique to help you feel the right rhythm. Imagine yourself jumping up, your legs stretching slowly as you gain height; at the top of the jump you seem to float and then finally you sink softly downwards, allowing your legs to fold under you as you absorb the landing and prepare for the next jump. Use words to help with the timing: *juuummmmmppp aaannndddd siiiinnnkk, juuummmmmppp*

aaannnddd siiiinnnkk. Breathing is important, concentrate on exhaling on the sink. Start the next run in the same way and once the rhythm has established itself land with your heels very slightly to one side so that you do a very small turn. The secret here is to do tiny turns; most skiers attempting these for the first time tend to try to turn their skis too much and consequently lose control and fall over.

Falling over in the powder rarely hurts and providing your clothing is adequate it does not even have to be unpleasant. Most people do not mind falling over, but do get very tired and frustrated when they try to get going again. Getting back up after a fall can be difficult, so try crossing your poles and putting your hand on the crossed part

85

to push up with – this will give you more support than the normal way. When you come to put the skis back on, clear all the snow from the bindings and make a platform for the downhill ski in the snow just above you. Scrape the snow from the boot sole either by using the other ski or by using your poles. Now, by crossing your downhill leg in front of you, put on the ski. Replacing the uphill ski can be done in two ways: you can repeat the procedure for the downhill ski although it will not be necessary to cross the legs, or you can place the ski in a T-shape with its tail resting against the middle of your downhill foot and the tip uphill of you. Dust yourself off, clear the inevitable snow-filled goggles and away you go again. Actually turning to face down the fall-line can present difficulties, if so try digging the heels of your skis into the snow with the tips facing outwards and keeping the skis horizontal so that you do not slide down. When you are comfortable and facing down the slope in this way, a gentle rock forwards should allow you to slide away in control.

If you are falling over a lot it will probably be because your timing of the jumps is too rapid, so try to vary the rhythm and see if that helps. Even more likely is that you will be turning your feet too much, so try them with hardly any turn at all. When you reach the bottom and look at your tracks you will be surprised at just how much the skis have been turning. If you are still having no luck it could be that the slope is too shallow and you are not building up enough speed to allow the skis to plane or float up towards the surface during the jump phase.

If your parallel turns are a little uncertain at the best of times it may be wise to try some stem turns first. Do them with a strong up and down motion and use as much stem as you are comfortable with; enjoyment is the main criterion. As your confidence grows and the rhythm improves, so you will be able to make do with less and less stem. If a member of your party gets tired or hurts themselves to the extent that they are having great trouble getting down, you can help by doing long stem turns with the stem phase lasting until you reach the new traverse line. They can then ski in the relative comfort of your tracks.

As you begin to master the jump turns you will want to progress to steeper slopes, and as you do so you will need to edge the skis more and more. This will result in a build-up of pressure under the base of the ski, causing it to flex and turn. Your turns will become bouncier than ever, so much so that the skis will often leave the snow totally during the jump phase. It is now time for you to try some other types of turns.

Repeat these very edgy dynamic turns, but as the skis are about to leave the snow try to let them drift over the surface; as they begin to dive into the next turn, extend your legs powerfully and then relax and you will begin to feel the skis shooting to the surface again. These are compression turns. A more conventional approach would be to return to the shallow slope and to descend it in a schuss, but this time we will push our legs deeper and then pull them up again just as though we were skiing through the moguls. Imagine that there is a line of moguls in front of you and ski through them trying to keep your head and body level. When you have successfully done this a few times introduce some small turns. Again, make sure they are very small at first. As you progress to steeper terrain remember to over-edge the skis if you are experiencing any problems. Breath-

Fig 66   This technique can be used in any difficult conditions.

(i) Move the uphill ski out into the stemmed position, pressurising it as much as possible throughout. If you cannot move the uphill ski easily, move both skis. Do not be in a rush to complete the stemming action, allow the skis to flow.

(ii) Hold the skis in the plough position for as long as is necessary, while they are in this position they will clear a track in which those behind can ski more easily.

(iii) Return to the traverse position.

Compression turns in the powder

(i) With your skis deep in the powder and edged, allow them to come to the surface.

(ii) Pole plant. Pull your knees to your chest, allowing the skis to float over the surface.

(iii) Extend strongly and edge the skis, making them do the work of turning.

(iv) Prepare to relax your legs, and as the skis begin to come to the surface use your thigh and stomach muscles again to control them.

Fig 67

Fig 68 Compression turns in the powder.

ing is very important and you should exhale as you extend your legs. Your pole plant will also help with the timing and it occurs at the same point as when you are skiing the bumps – on the crest of the bump when your legs are bent to the maximum. This is one of the most versatile and enjoyable ways of skiing the deep and has really superseded the old method of banking, although this too can be fun. Banking is a technique that allows you to edge the skis and keep the feet together. Start just as before, but lean or bank your body into the turn; you will see mono-skiers doing this all the time.

So far in the deep snow I have been encouraging you to over-edge the skis even though you will not be able to feel the edges biting, but now as you begin to ski a little faster this action may cause the skis to turn and dive too much and you will begin to lose control in a fairly dramatic manner. If you have experienced this it is time for you to experiment with the surf turn, as this turn allows you to control the edges of the ski more precisely. A good way to learn this turn is to take out a monoski, but failing that (having tried them first in the way I described previously) choose a steep slope, ski it with the compression turns you have already been using and allow the speed to increase. As the skis float to the surface adopt the surf technique and do not edge the skis so much; you will find that you can now handle the increase in speed, at least physically if not mentally. As your confidence grows start to experiment with different turning techniques, in particular try the hip rolling and the knee rolling turns.

If you want to be really radical try some straight-lining, in this case the barriers are purely mental. Where others have turned, you just lean back and go straight for as long as your legs, the terrain or your nerves will allow. Once you have mastered the basics be creative, there is a whole new world waiting for off-the-lips, aerial re-entrys, and so on. Anything goes providing you are enjoying it and not endangering yourself or others.

Bottomless Powder

Unfortunately true bottomless powder is a rarity in the Alps, but if you are lucky enough to experience it you should employ the same techniques as for the light and deep snows. You will not feel any base at all so you must be very sensitive to the pressures under your feet in order to maintain your balance. Compression turns are usually the most successful, and if you add the foot thrusting technique we looked at earlier you will be skiing just like the stars of those ski films.

Heavy Snows

Heavy snows occur in two different ways: the first as wet snowfalls and the second as a result of a rise in the ambient temperature. Whatever the cause, the result is the same – a wet, heavy mass which is admirably described by the term 'porridge'. The problem with trying to ski it is that it compresses easily at first then solidifies suddenly and unpredictably, and any sort of pivoting action becomes very

difficult if your skis are still in the snow. If it is deep the problem is intensified because your boots then offer even more resistance to turning. The techniques are more or less the same whether the snow is deep or shallow, it is only the degree of the actions that change. The only exception to this is found when skiing steep terrain.

Stem turns are not easy in these conditions because they involve a pivoting action. If, however, you step the ski into its stemmed position instead of pushing it, this will ease the problem. This stepping action may have to be quite large and, in fact, the whole turn might have to be a combination of a stem turn and the 1,000 step turn, depending on the snow.

Stepping turns are a good survival technique although their effectiveness will depend upon the extent to which you can lift your ski and boot clear of the snow. Whether you lift the tip, tail or the whole ski again depends upon the depth of the snow and the steepness of the slope. Having practised all three you should be in a position to experiment and find out which is the most appropriate system to use. It usually only takes a step or two of experimentation to find out!

Jump turns are particularly good on steeper terrain, but on shallow slopes tend to be very tiring. When you jump, make sure that your skis leave the surface thus allowing you to rotate them freely. One way of making these turns less tiring is to use the terrain to help with the jumps. Look for small bumps which will help you to get some air. A powerful yet subtle leg action will be required on landing; if you try any rapid movement you run the risk of injuring yourself. Land as softly as possible to maintain good balance and to prevent the skis digging in too far, which would make it more difficult to complete the turn. It follows that the less you actually turn the better; the closer you can ski to the flow-line the less rotation needed. Also, the faster you ski the more likely the skis are to float to the surface where they are obviously easier to turn. As they do this the jump phase becomes more difficult and will eventually, at a certain speed, disappear; it is then time to employ the compression turn. Before we look at this, however, let's just mention the short swings that can be used in steep heavy snow.

If you are strong enough to push the skis around the swing phase of the turn, you can use short swings that are rotated about the front of the skis. The point of rotation will be related to the depth of the snow and the angle of the slope. As the slope gets steeper and deeper, so your weight will move backwards. The pressure on your feet will move from the balls of your feet to the heels. There will come a point at which it is definitely desirable to turn about the heels of the skis. It may even be necessary to thrust the feet forwards to clear the boots of the snow. Once forwards they can be rotated in a windscreen-wiper action, which also allows the tails to slice through the snow. This turn was used extensively in many difficult snow conditions by that master of extreme skiing, Sylvain Saudan. Plenty of anticipation, which is pre-turning the upper body in the direction you are about to go, will help with these turns.

It is always difficult to know just how much to turn the skis on any particular turn, because you do not know what the consistency will be on landing. There are two techniques that may help. The first is to test the snow with your pole plant, if it does not feel right do not proceed with the turn, but test it again with another pole plant and so on until you find some suitable snow. The second method relates to the windscreen-wiper turns; as you do them allow the skis to become airborne and as you land do so on the heels and feel the snow with the tails of your skis. Depending on the sensation you get, you will either rotate the skis further or reduce the amount. This technique requires many miles of skiing before you are able to respond quickly enough, but don't despair – it only needs practice.

Now back to our friend the compression turn; I call it our friend because as you will begin to see it is probably the most versatile off-piste technique. The advantage of compression turns in these conditions is that they make it possible to ski very smoothly, avoiding sudden twists and turns and to keep the skis close to the surface. Again, the faster you are prepared to ski the easier it will be, although obviously the chances of injury are also increased (I will not dwell on this point though, as a positive attitude is vital). It will probably be necessary in the deep heavy snows to lean back to allow the skis to come to the surface, and this is one of the rare occasions that I recommend you to do so.

If you apply too much edge the ski may turn too sharply, throwing you off balance. These conditions are therefore ideal for exponents of the surf technique, since the subtle application of the edge that is possible with this type of turn is a definite advantage. Look for terrain contours as these can help considerably, and if you are skiing quite fast and the slope is not too steep you could try hip-rolling turns as these also allow you to keep the pressure under your skis consistent and are subtle enough for you not to be suddenly thrown off balance.

(a)

(b)

(c)

Fig 69   Oops!

92

Fig 70 Superb powder skiing; notice the amount of edge the skier is applying.

Heavy snow will demand a respectful approach from you, but with practice it need not be quite the ogre it appears to be when you first meet it. It is a form of real snow that will need some dedication to really come to terms with, but it is encountered frequently and, as I implied in the introduction, meeting the challenges that the real snow world throws at you is part of the fun, and this attittude is certainly needed to ski the next type – everybody's friend the crust!

Breakable Crust

This comes in two forms: crust that breaks as you ski it and crust that only does so inconsistently. Let's deal with the former first. If you think the crust is consistent, you have to decide whether it will break with every turn or whether it will remain intact. If you think it will stay intact, then foot-lifting turns or compression turns will work best. Both turns allow you to ski smoothly with subtle pressure changes, although you may have to adopt a gentler approach to your foot-lifting turns than normal. The foot-lifting turns are best if the surface is very hard and glazed, as these conditions present similar problems to ice. If you are doubtful about the crust's ability to hold your weight do not use this technique, as it could be quite dangerous if

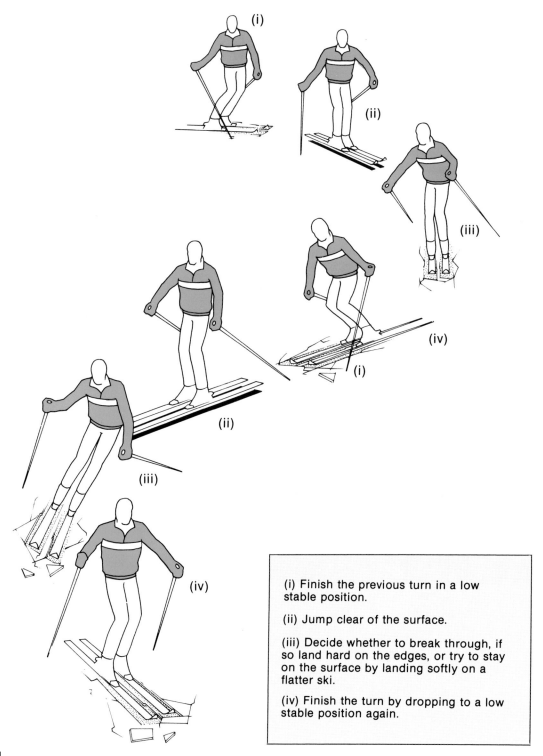

(i) Finish the previous turn in a low stable position.

(ii) Jump clear of the surface.

(iii) Decide whether to break through, if so land hard on the edges, or try to stay on the surface by landing softly on a flatter ski.

(iv) Finish the turn by dropping to a low stable position again.

Fig 71

Compression turns in the crust

(i) Pull your legs up, keep the skis flat (to distribute the weight) and the pressure even over both feet.

(ii) Decision time; a strong extension on an edged ski will break through, whilst a gentle, sensitive extension on a flat ski (using the surf technique) may keep the skis on the surface.

Fig 72

Fig 73   The Scottish Highlands offer excellent touring.

the crust does break. Whichever technique you adopt, you will need to ski with very light feet and be ultra-sensitive to the pressures under them. Surf technique is also valuable because it will allow greater control of the edges, and too much edge may cause the skis to break through.

When the crust is tending to break on the turns anyway, you must make sure that it does so on every turn. You can achieve this in several ways: try jump turns and as you land extend your legs powerfully to break through, similarly during the extension phase of the compression turn extend with more vigour than usual. Sometimes it will be necessary to use a strong foot thrusting movement to get the feet to the surface again to start the next turn. The faster you ski the more likely you are to

break through, and when it gets steep you can employ the same techniques as you did in the heavy snows.

Inconsistent crust is one of the most difficult snow types to ski and as such presents a great challenge to the skier of real snow. Approach it with a sense of humour and a feeling that if you get down you have been successful – any pretence of skiing it with style should be discarded immediately. The best approach is to ski it with very sensitive compression or surf turns. Look carefully at the surface, sometimes you will be able to anticipate where it will hold and where it will break according to the snow's colour or texture.

Sooner or later we all run out of patience in the crust and just want to get out of it by the easiest method. There are three survival methods you can try: traverses linked with kick turns, traverses linked with stem turns and the 1,000 step turn with the pressure usually having to be on the heels. If you are linking stem turns, test the ground with your pole plant and with the stemmed ski before you commit yourself to turning. On steep terrain simple middle pressured leg retraction short swings will work if you have the energy to maintain them, if you have not then you would not be the first to take off your skis and walk.

Spring Snow

After the beast comes the beauty – spring snow. There is very little to say about it because it is easy to ski and you can employ any of the techniques you have learned. Do not be confined by the regimen of techniques however, enjoy it in as carefree a fashion as you want.

Ice and Hardpack

For most of you I suspect that this condition is 'public enemy number two'. To survive it adopt a wide stance and sideslip down, slowing your speed by aiming for any patches of loose snow. To ski it you must have very sharp edges, have enough confidence and nerve to ski fast and you must also ski gently. You cannot ski ice and hardpack slowly because they do not allow you to skid the skis which is the way we kill the speed.

Choose your line so that you head for any patches of loose snow on which you will be able to lose some speed, and use the foot-lifting turns because they enable you to get on your edges early in the turn.

Gently does it is then the name of the game, as any sudden movements will cause you to lose the edge. Try using the whole edge of the ski, making the front part bite first and finishing on the tail. Achieve this by sliding your feet through the turn. If you do feel the edges breaking away, go immediately into the next turn; you may just hold it and if you do not then you will have lost nothing by trying.

If you are an aggressive skier you may prefer to descend with a series of short sharp turns where you feel the edge bite under your foot and immediately go on to the next turn. Both of these turns rely not only on correctly tuned skis but also on the right type of ski. A soft ski will always be very difficult to ski in these conditions and you will have to make the best of a bad job – and for once can justly blame your tools.

Mixed Terrain

By this I mean snow that has been cut up by other skiers, old avalanche debris and generally any crud that has not yet been covered. The basic principle here is that if you are in a low position and on your edges you are stable. If you are gliding on a flat ski you could be knocked over more easily, so short turns going from edge to edge are the best to employ.

The Steep

Skiing the steep is really about an attitude of mind rather than techniques. When you *feel* ready you will *be* ready. However, the following are a few hints.

The basic ski turn used is the leg retraction short swing, although some of

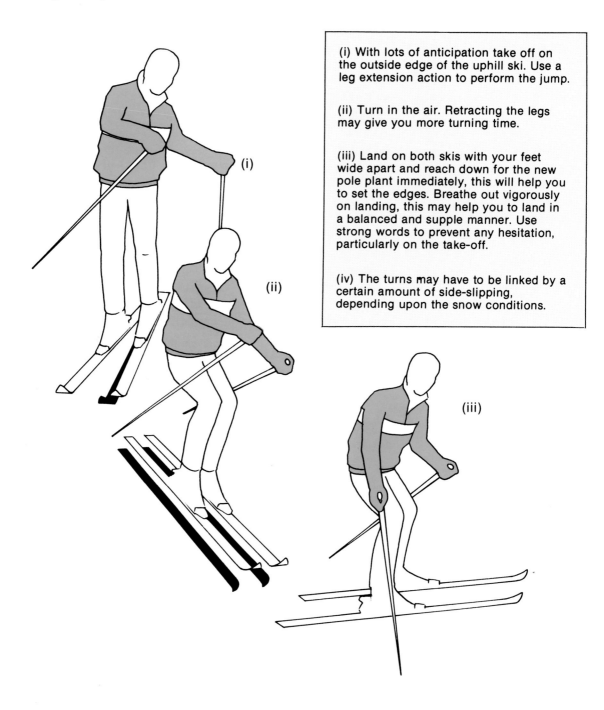

(i) With lots of anticipation take off on the outside edge of the uphill ski. Use a leg extension action to perform the jump.

(ii) Turn in the air. Retracting the legs may give you more turning time.

(iii) Land on both skis with your feet wide apart and reach down for the new pole plant immediately, this will help you to set the edges. Breathe out vigorously on landing, this may help you to land in a balanced and supple manner. Use strong words to prevent any hesitation, particularly on the take-off.

(iv) The turns may have to be linked by a certain amount of side-slipping, depending upon the snow conditions.

Fig 74

Fig 75 Glacier skiing.

Fig 76 The weather can quickly change, causing very difficult and dangerous conditions.

the modern exponents of extreme skiing advocate a short swing where you take off on the uphill ski. As you land use both skis, as this gives you a wider base, and immediately plant your pole as far down the slope as you can reach. This serves two functions: firstly it helps you to angulate and secondly it provides a third point to your landing base. Pole baskets that are soft, and will therefore bend to the angle of the slope, are essential if you are to avoid the pole plant skidding away. Slopes as steep as 60 degrees are now being skied, and to put that into perspective the average black run is only about 30 degrees. This level of skiing demands the utmost both mentally and physically of the skier and it is the preserve of a few, because on many of the slopes they are skiing to slip is to die.

99

The last two conditions that I will deal with are not connected to the snow, but can nevertheless cause a certain amount of anxiety.

Bad Visibility

All of you will, no doubt, have experienced the condition known as white-out, where you really cannot tell which way is which. The problem is that we have nothing to relate to, or so it would seem. We are over-reliant upon our sense of sight; the blind skier is always skiing in a white-out but their other senses are more highly developed. We must learn from their example and use other sources for feedback.

Our sense of feel through our feet can tell us what the terrain is doing, and by letting our poles drag along the ground we can sense how fast we are going and how much we are leaning. Listen to the sound of your edges scraping over the surface and feel the draught caused by your movement on your face. With practice you can, like the blind skier, develop these senses. Compression turns allow you to feel the terrain and edgy jump turns or stem turns help you keep the speed down and feel the surface.

Skiing in the Trees

Skiers of real snow can frequently find themselves amongst the trees, in fact it is a good place to head when the visibility is bad. It can also collect some excellent powder because it will be sheltered from the wind. The only problem is that there are often nasty tree roots and sawn-off trunks lurking for the unsuspecting skier. If you are in doubt about the snow's depth ski keeping the tips at the surface of the snow so that they cannot catch. Detach your hands from the ski pole straps so that if they get caught you do not wrench your shoulder.

When you ski in the trees it is important to adopt the right approach so that the trees do not intimidate you. When good skiers ski through any sort of obstacles they look at the slope in a particular way. Instead of looking at the slope and seeing trees, they will look and see the gaps between the trees. A slalom skier will likewise see the gaps between the poles not the poles themselves. This may sound like a minor point, but in fact it makes a very real difference to the line that you choose. Instead of skiing up to the tree and then turning, which means you will have left the turn too late, it forces you to turn much earlier and therefore allows you to ski past the obstacle with time to spare.

All the aforementioned techniques and hints are just guidelines designed to help you enjoy this off-piste game. They are not absolutes, and even if you can already ski some of the conditions have a go at trying to ski them in a different way. I believe the best skiers are those who are most versatile. Part of the fun of skiing real snow is the variety of conditions we meet and the variety of techniques and styles that we can use to cope with them. I hope these ideas will help you to enjoy your skiing more in the future, and stimulate you to try some new approaches.

5 Monoskiing

Monoskiing is fun and, moreover, the mono is so well suited to real snow that you do not have to be an expert to be able to use it. The techniques needed in the main bear little resemblance to normal skiing, in fact one could argue that free expression is what monoskiing is all about. For this reason I will only tell you enough to get you started and then the rest is up to you.

The ski should be about head height; it does not need to be as long as your normal skis. All the other equipment is standard, although some people carry a very short ski clamped between their boots to assist them on the tows. For your first attempt choose a day that has good visibility and deep snow; monoskis are quite hard to handle on-piste.

Your first problem is getting to the powder. If possible take a chair-lift. Leave one foot free to help you to manoeuvre into position and when you are on the chair put the other boot into the binding. If the exit from the lift is steep and icy, then I hope your companion on the chair is understanding!

Picked yourself up? Good, it is fun – honestly! Now head for the deep snow as quickly as possible. If getting there involves skiing the piste for a while the surf turns you have been learning will be useful, otherwise ski as normally as possible. Initially you will probably find the tail breaking away all the time and this will have the effect of sending you around in circles. Once you begin to relax and stand centrally on your ski this problem will disappear. If you have to traverse then positively pulling up with the downhill leg will help. However, the monoski is not designed for traversing on hard snows and this manoeuvre is always tricky. It helps to have a friend with you, if for nothing more but to join in the jollity.

Having finally reached the deep snow you have done the hard bit. Do not despair or even entertain the idea of giving up at this stage, life now gets easier. Point the ski downhill and go. You can turn using a variety of techniques: you can just lean to the side or do surf turns or compression turns or whatever you like – anything goes.

If you fall over, getting back up can be a little tricky. Remember the trick I showed you with the crossed poles? Now is the time to use it. Another way is to position the ski underneath you so that you are sitting on the back of it, point it downhill and off you go again. When it has picked up a little speed, pull yourself upright and continue skiing.

Now you have reached the bottom and the only way up is via a drag lift. We are in for some entertainment! I remember my first attempt very clearly; I grabbed the Poma, put it between my legs and off I shot. After about two metres (2 yards) I felt my balance going, but I was determined not to lose face in front of the crowd of pisteurs that had gathered for some fun at my expense. So I jumped up in an effort to gain some semblance of control, did two 360's and, to my amaze-

Fig 77 Banking.

Fig 78   Normal techniques can be ignored, develop your own style.

Fig 79   Air time on a mono.

ment, landed straight on the track again. There were cheers of approval from my onlookers, but my jubilation was short-lived – around the next corner I fell off completely! I skied down amidst much laughter to try again. There is no easy solution to this problem other than carrying the short ski I mentioned earlier. If you don't have one of these, the best advice I can offer is to go up with the ski skidding diagonally across the track and to keep a sense of humour! Better still, to plan your day with the help of the piste map and to avoid the drags altogether.

After a couple of attempts why not try straight-lining? You have probably seen the experts do it in the films: they lean back, arching their spines, with their hands held out flamboyantly to the sides. It really is not very difficult to do: the tail digs in and the sole of the ski catches the air so that it lifts right up, and then it is only your nerve that has to hold steady as you streak straight down the slope.

I will say no more about this aspect of skiing real snow. When the conditions are suitable give it a go; I am sure you will have a lot of fun.

6 Snowsurfing

There are a number of snowsurfing boards on the market at the moment; the designs vary slightly but they all operate in more or less the same way. The techniques needed to use them bear no relationship to conventional skiing; if, however, you have surfed or skateboarded you should have little trouble adapting those skills to snowsurfing. Like with the monoski, I only intend to give you enough information to get you started, because I do not want to bog you down with technique and I believe that this is another area where free expression is the name of the game.

There are as many different ideas about designs as there are designs; whichever you have the opportunity to try, ensure that the foot fixing arrangement is secure and that the leash is also strong and secure. You can wear après ski boots or Alpine mountaineering boots. Après ski boots, if they are warm enough, are generally more supple around the foot and for that reason I prefer them. Getting to and from the deep snow can be awkward unless the resort has a good chair-lift system. However, you can buy very small skis that do not require ski boots and bindings and you could use these to travel on the button lifts.

Snowsurfing is definitely a deep soft snow game, as the boards are very difficult to control on any piste or hard surface. For your first attempts choose a day that has good visibility and some nice powder. Head for a slope that has about the same gradient as a green or blue run, because the first thing that you will realise is that snowsurfing is fast, I certainly always feel as though I am going faster than normal. The slope must also run out properly because there is nothing worse than finding you have no gradient left and have to walk. Walking in deep soft snow is extremely tiring and has nothing to recommend it at all.

There are two different stances on a snow board: if you lead with your left foot you have a natural stance and if with the right foot you have a goofy stance. Despite the derogatory name, goofy footers are at no disadvantage. Adopt the stance that feels most comfortable for you. Steering is simple: to go to the right lean to the right and to go to the left lean to the left. If you are facing the way you are turning it is known as a frontside turn, and a backside turn is when your back is to the turn. Try to distribute your weight evenly over both feet; the most common error is to stand too much on the rear foot.

To start I usually face the slope, make a platform for the board, stand on it and then either swivel or jump it into the fall-line and away I go. If you have chosen a shallow slope you should be able to stick to the flow-line doing a number of snaky turns by just flexing your ankles, as you pick up more speed so you can begin to bank into the turns. Keep your legs bent, as this will give you more control and also lower your centre of gravity which in turn makes you more stable. The surfers' pose with their arms out wide is also functional

Fig 80   The flamboyance of the monoskier.

Fig 81   A front-side turn on a snow board.

Fig 82   Anything goes.

because it again helps with your balance. All your movements should be as smooth as possible and at first you should go for long elegant turns. Falls tend to be frequent and spectacular but not in the least bit serious.

Once you have found your balance and have mastered the standard frontside and backside turns, look for some more interesting terrain. Gulleys and banks offer endless fun and the limitations are only in your mind. If the conditions are right and you are with a good crowd of friends I can guarantee that you will experience one of your most memorable days in the mountains.

7　Ski Touring

As ski slopes become increasingly crowded, so more and more people are turning to the game of ski touring to escape the throngs. Many believe that the effort needed to climb up merely enhances our enjoyment and appreciation of the mountains. Originally ski touring was the preserve of the mountaineer, but as it has attracted a more diverse following so the emphasis has moved away from just using the skis to travel and climb peaks. Many now use ski touring techniques in order to reach good skiing, that being their primary objective rather than the ascent of the mountain. It is not for me to pass any judgement on the relative merits of these two aspects of the sport, only to point out the directions in which it is moving.

Ski touring can be enjoyed at many levels, but as soon as you move above the tree line it is essential that you appreciate the severity of this environment. I suggest, therefore, that unless you are an experienced winter mountaineer or Alpinist you employ the services of a qualified Guide or go with very experienced friends. Not only are you confronted with the usual hazards of the avalanche, but also with the problems of navigation, safeguarding steep terrain, the use of crampons and ice-axe, and the problems associated with travelling in glaciated terrain. I am not trying to put you off, but it would be irresponsible of me to encourage you to partake in this very satisfying aspect of skiing real snow without making you aware of the needs of the sport. This chapter will familiarise you with the required techniques, but you should practise them under the watchful eye of an experienced friend. There are many variations to those I have described, but if you are conversant with these you will be able to operate safely.

Uphill Techniques

These are the techniques that will allow you to move into a new world full of long empty powder slopes and high mountain peaks. Many enjoy the thrill of climbing up, whilst to others it is a necessary evil; whichever group you fall into the following points should help to make life easier. We examined the tools of the trade earlier, so let's now learn how to use them.

First you need to apply your skins. Dry the base of the ski as best you can; this can be quite difficult in a storm, but you should make every effort as it will save you problems later. If it is a skin with a hook, fix it to the tail first, making sure it sticks firmly as you go. When you reach halfway, fix the front in position then press firmly down on the skin along its whole length. Avoid getting any snow on the glue as it will not stick if you do. Skins without a hook must be started at the front; if you have difficulty making the tail end stick you can use an elastic band or a specially designed hook which can be added to this type of skin. In some snows it may be necessary to rub wax into the skin to prevent the snow from sticking. It may

Fig 83   Relaxing in an Alpine hut during a tour. These huts are situated high up in the mountains and it is possible to go many days without returning to a village.

also be worth doing this if you have a lot of moderate climbing to do, as it helps the ski to glide.

With your skins applied to the base of your skis and the bindings in the uphill mode find a flat piece of snow. Practise walking along with a sliding action, moving your arms and poles as you would when walking normally. Try to develop the feeling that you are gliding along a little with each step. Lifting the skis will only tire you, so develop this gliding action before venturing uphill. Another way to reduce fatigue is to develop a rhythm, stopping only where the terrain dictates or after maybe an hour, depending on your level of fitness.

When you have mastered this, start to

go uphill. Easy slopes can be tackled in the same way, but as the angle increases you will find it necessary to take a diagonal traverse, the steepness of which will depend upon the snow and your technique. Initially you will be able to turn at the end of each traverse by doing simple small steps uphill until you reach a more comfortable angle. Eventually, however, the slope will steepen to a point where this becomes impossible. It is now time to employ the infamous kick turn. Years ago every skier learned these very early in their ski careers regardless of their future intentions, but now many will never have been shown how to do them properly.

There are two types of kick turn, the uphill kick turn and the downhill kick

Fig 84   Ascending a steep slope, the skier is holding the pole at half height to save straining his arm.

Downhill kick turns

Fig 85　The importance of the leader levelling out a platform cannot be overstressed as it makes a considerable difference to the ease with which this manoeuvre can be performed. Standing level (or even slightly downhill if your skis do not slide), place your poles in firmly behind you.

Fig 86　Lift the downhill ski, resting the tail lightly on the snow in front of your uphill foot.

Fig 87　Allow the ski to fall to the other side, keeping control of it throughout. Bring the pole around to help with your balance.

Fig 88　Standing on the outside edge of this ski, lift the remaining ski into position and remove the poles. Be very careful not to sit down on the snow at any stage, as this will almost certainly lead to an unpleasant slide down the hill.

Uphill kick turns

Fig 89   In this instance the platform should be as steep in the direction of the traverse as the security of the skis will allow.

Fig 90   Place the poles in firmly, lift the uphill ski and place it in the new direction.

Fig 91   Standing positively on the inside edge of the newly placed ski, bring the old downhill ski to its new uphill position, removing the poles as you do so.

turn, and there is much debate amongst tourers as to which is the most appropriate. I tend to use the uphill most of the time because it allows me to continue with my rhythm, and employ the downhill version only when the snow is very deep or when on steep slopes. Before I explain how best to learn these two techniques, let me first illustrate how not to learn them. In the formative years of my skiing career I was fortunate enough to ski with a number of experienced mountaineers whose joy was off-piste skiing. They were very patient and dragged me everywhere enjoying, I think, the spectacle of me developing the exclamation mark turn – straight down fall (!), straight down fall (!). On one particular occasion they spotted a beautiful untouched powder bowl, my questions about why it had remained untouched were met by a whoop and a cloud of powder as they shot off down. When I finally arrived at the bottom by my usual technique all I could find were a set of tracks. I followed them until to my horror they disappeared over a cliff. Before my imagination went wild with images of them jumping over this precipice I spotted them down below. 'Just side slip down the runnel' they shouted, neglecting to tell me that it was icy. I teetered down only to be met by a blank wall of rock. 'What now?' I shouted. 'Kick turn round and go the other way,' they replied. 'What's a kick turn?' came the inevitable reply. As they fell about in the snow, I could not quite decide whether it was in dismay or because they were laughing so much. The rest is, I am glad to say, history and I suggest you find more amicable surroundings in which to practise your first kick turns.

When ascending a slope the leader should level out the tracks at each change of direction, thus creating a platform on which to turn. Once you have done a few easy angled slopes, find a short steep but safe slope and see how steeply you can go up. You will need to use the climbers and make small steps ensuring that you distribute the pressure evenly over the whole ski base. If you experience difficulties you are probably either rolling your foot forwards and not keeping the pressure on the climber or rolling your foot slightly to one side and on to the edge rather than the skin. Use your poles for balance and hold the uphill pole on the shaft to avoid your shoulder aching. With practice you will be surprised at how steeply the skins will grip. If the conditions are very hard or icy you will have to use the harschisen. Remember that if they are attached to the binding they will not work if you use the climber, so you may also have to adopt a shallower traverse. In extremely hard conditions it may be necessary to stamp the harschisen down to make them bite. If you come across anything steeper or harder you will have to use ice-axe and crampons.

Ice-axe

The ice-axe has a multitude of uses in the mountains and every ski tourer should carry one and be conversant with the techniques needed to use it. We will look at the three most important uses in detail, self-arrest, step cutting and anchoring, but first we must look at how to carry the axe. When you are skiing through crevassed terrain it must be easily accessible for reasons that will become obvious when we examine crevasse rescue. The easiest place to store it is between your shoulder-blades

Fig 92 Carrying your ice-axe. Slide it between the straps, your back and the rucksack.

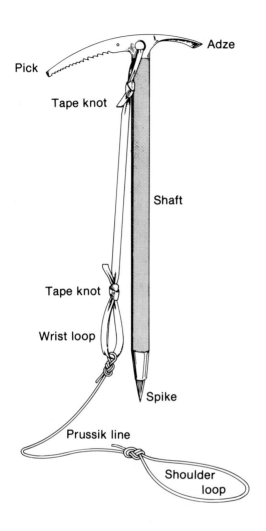

Fig 93 The ice-axe. Make sure the retaining sling is long enough to allow the axe to be used at arm's length with both hands.

Labels on figure: Pick, Adze, Tape knot, Shaft, Tape knot, Wrist loop, Spike, Prussik line, Shoulder loop

Self-arrest

Self-arrest is a system by which you can stop yourself after a fall and it must be practised. Find a steep concave slope of hard snow which has a safe run-out. Ideally you should wear old waterproofs, gloves and a climber's helmet to protect yourself; do not use any crampons at this stage. Follow the sequence in Figs 94 to 97. When you are confident try it wearing your skis and sack.

Once you have mastered all these techniques you should feel more confident on steep terrain. It is important to be aware, however, that even with good technique and a cool head it can be very difficult to stop yourself on slopes above 40 degrees.

Step Cutting

Step cutting, even amongst many mountaineers, is a sadly neglected skill. Many of our most spectacular peaks were originally climbed by climbers cutting thousands of steps. The technique was superseded by the crampon, but is still of value in case you lose or break a crampon. Fig 98 illustrates the various methods; do take time out to practise the skill as you never know when you might need it.

Self-belaying

Finally, you can use the axe to anchor yourself to the mountain. When you are climbing up or down place the axe firmly into the snow before you move, then if your feet slip you can hold on to the axe for support. This is known as self-belaying and provides a safe technique for moving quickly over fairly steep ground. You can use the axe to anchor with in several other ways which I will look at in detail later.

and the sack. This sounds uncomfortable, but in fact is not. I always have the axe tied to a length of rope which forms a sling, which in turn is passed around my shoulders so that I cannot drop the axe. When you are climbing with the axe you can either have the adze towards you, which is more comfortable, or away from you, which means the axe is then in the right position for self-arrest.

Fig 94   Self-arrest; basic position. (i) Ice-axe head under your shoulder. (ii) Cover the spike with your hand. (iii) Feet raised. (iv) Apply the pick gradually to reduce the chances of it being snatched from your grasp. Lifting your hips will apply further pressure.

Fig 95   Self-arrest; on your back (head first). (i) Reach to the side placing the axe in such a way as to cause you to rotate to a feet-first position. (ii) Roll over into the basic position.

(a)

(b)

Fig 96 Self-arrest; on your back (feet first). Roll towards the head of the axe
returning to the basic position.

Fig 97   Self-arrest; on your stomach (head first).
(i) Reach as far out to the side as you can with
the axe; this will cause you to rotate. (ii) If the
snow is very hard remove the axe and replace it
as for the basic position. This double action
will prevent the axe being pulled from your grasp.

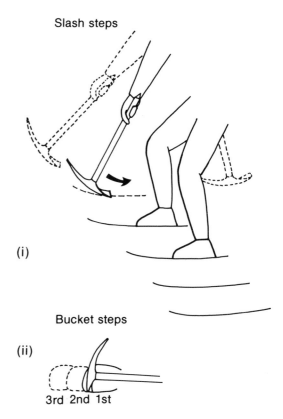

Fig 98   Step cutting.
(i) The easiest type of step is the slash step. This
is cut by swinging the axe hand in such an arc
that the adze cuts cleanly through the snow. The
arm should be kept straight, and with practice it
should take no more than two swings per step.
Work diagonally up the slope, anticipating each
step forwards. If you are descending, you will
need to cut two steps in front of you so that you
can descend without crossing your legs, as this
would cause the boot to roll out of the step.
(ii) For larger steps you will need to cut a bucket
step. Cut a hole with the adze and then cut the
next hole into this one.

Crampons

Cramponing should be practised first on
easy terrain so that you get used to wearing
them. I am not going to teach you how to
go up vertical faces as that is beyond the
scope of this book and the type of crampon
that most of us carry for touring is not
suitable for this usage. The main thing to
remember is to walk with your toes
slightly apart so that you do not spike your
own calf muscles and try to get as many
spikes into the snow as possible. Slacken
your boots so that your ankles are as

flexible as possible; this will allow you to
keep your feet flat against the surface even
when it gets quite steep. In some snow
conditions the snow will stick to the
crampons, balling up underneath. This
condition can be quite hazardous and the
snow should be cleared by either kicking
hard into the next step or by knocking
your boot with the ice-axe shaft.

Fig 99 Cramponing with flexible ankles.

This is not an exhaustive list of techniques, but it covers all the situations that you are likely to come across on normal tours. For more advanced techniques I feel you should follow a course of instruction from qualified people.

Ropework

Those of you unused to handling ropes, prepare for some mind-twisting fun! I have kept the number of knots that you have to learn to a minimum and with a little perseverance you should soon master them. They can be learned in the comfort of your home and indeed it is far better that you familiarise yourself with them

there than half-way down a crevasse!

The techniques that I have described are those needed to operate in crevassed terrain and to protect someone who is about to test-ski a potential avalanche slope. I have not described the ropework needed to ascend and descend rock ridges, or steep snow and ice, as I feel that these situations are beyond the normal concept of ski touring. If, however, you are interested in these skills you should refer to the bibliography for details.

The Rope

Basically, there are two types of rope available: hawserlaid rope and kernmantle rope. The former, although cheaper, is rarely used nowadays because it is much harder to handle, so I will confine myself to discussing the kernmantle variety.

Let's start by considering the length of the rope. If you buy a climbing rope it will normally come in two lengths: 45 metres and 50 metres. If you are skiing in a party of two or three I think it is essential that you use the 50 metre length. The reasons for this will become evident when you read the section on crevasse rescue. If you are skiing in a larger party, providing you have at least 9 metres of rope between each person you should be safe. Large parties may decide to cut their rope into short convenient lengths thereby spreading the load throughout the group, this does, however, reduce the versatility of the rope.

Climbing ropes generally come in three diameters: 11mm, 9mm and 7mm. The first is usually considered to be too thick and heavy for touring, and I feel that the last, although strong enough, can be difficult to prussik up (prussiking, as you will see, is one of the major rescue methods)

Coiling the rope

Fig 100 Holding both ends, pull through three lengths.

Fig 101 Coil each subsequent length into a loop, making sure each loop is in the same direction. With this method there is no need to worry about the twisting that will occur.

Fig 102 When you reach the middle, use the spare rope to wind around the hank.

Fig 103 After three wraps, pull a loop through the hank.

Fig 104   Pass this loop over the top of the hank.

Fig 105   Pull the spare rope tight. The spare can either be wrapped around the rest of the hank or used as 'rucksack straps' to carry the rope. With the hank on your back pass each rope over a shoulder, around your back and tie the two ends together around your waist. This method is quick, easy and, in spite of the apparent mess, will not cause any tangles.

and so my own preference is for 50 metres of 9mm kernmantle.

For the expenditure of a little extra money you can get ropes that have been treated to prevent them soaking up water. This makes sense because a wet rope is an extremely heavy item to carry on a tour.

There are a number of different ways to coil a rope, but I have only illustrated one as I believe that it is perfectly adequate for our situation. The rope should be stored away from direct sunlight and should always be dried naturally. Respect your rope: do not stand on it in ski boots or in skis, and replace it according to the manufacturer's recommendations. Finally, do not be tempted to buy or use anything but a proper climbing rope. Climbing ropes are specially constructed to survive the rigours we subject them to and they

will carry a UIAA label identifying them as such.

Slings and Karabiners

Each party member should carry two 8 foot 1 inch (120 × 19mm) tapes (strength is 2,500kg). These can be of the sewn variety or you can tie them with the tape knot, do not try to sew them yourself. Every member should also carry four 2,500kg screwgate karabiners (UIAA approved), one of which should be the pear-shaped or HMS variety, one pulley and two prussik loops.

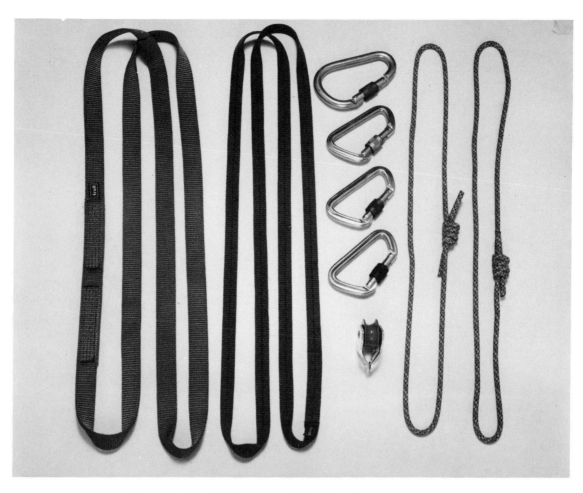

Fig 106 Equipment; two 8 foot slings, four 2,500kg screwgate karabiners (one pear-shaped), one pulley and two prussik loops (using 1.5 metres of line).

Harnesses

The advantage of wearing a harness over just tying the rope around your waist is that there is then no chance of the rope riding up over your diaphragm causing you to asphyxiate. There is, however, the extra cost and weight to consider. Before the advent of harnesses tourers either carried a prussik already attached to the rope that they could stand in or they constructed a harness out of the rope.

There are two types of harness available: the UIAA approved full body harness or the lighter sit harness. Sit harnesses do not have approval because in the event of a

fall they do not allow the subject to hang in the best possible position. However, with the method of tying on to the rope that I will show you this problem is easily overcome. Whichever you choose, keep it light and simple and preferably of a design that has leg loops which undo so that it can be put on over ski boots.

Knots

Figs 107 to 116 illustrate the absolute minimum of knots that you will need to be able to cope with the types of situation met in ski touring. They can and should be practised at home. There is nothing worse than fumbling around in the cold trying to remember knots. Practise them with your mitts on until tying them becomes second nature. The usage of the knots will become evident as you read on.

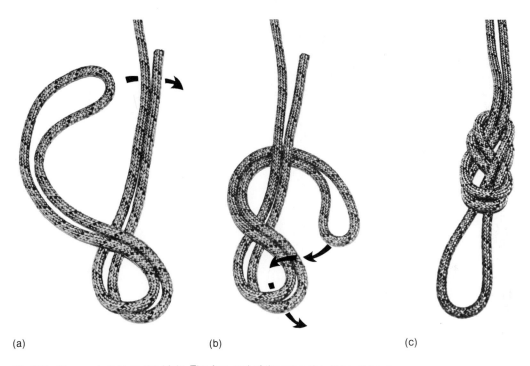

(a)　　　　　　　　(b)　　　　　　　　(c)

Fig 107　Figure-of-eight on the bight. The free end of the rope should be at least 20cm (8 inches long).

Clove hitch

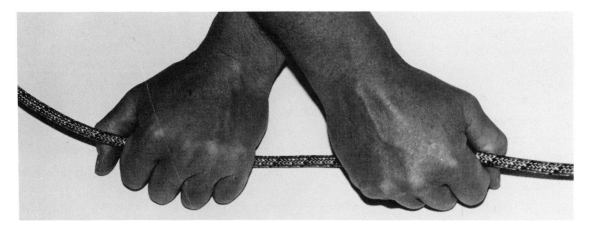

Fig 108　Cross your hands and grasp the rope.

Fig 109   Uncross your hands.

Fig 110   Cross your hands again in the other direction.

Fig 111 Grasp both loops in one hand and clip the karabiner into them.

Fig 112 The finished knot. There are many ways of tying a clove hitch, but this one is fairly foolproof.

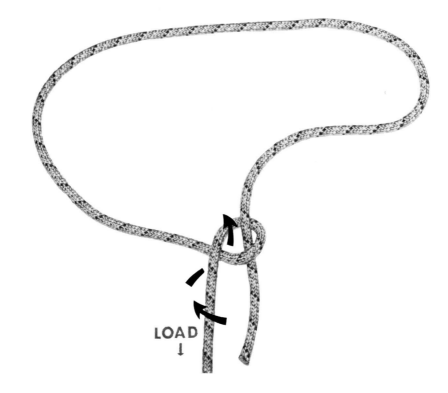

(a)

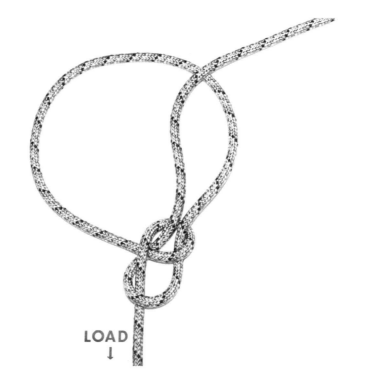

(b)

126

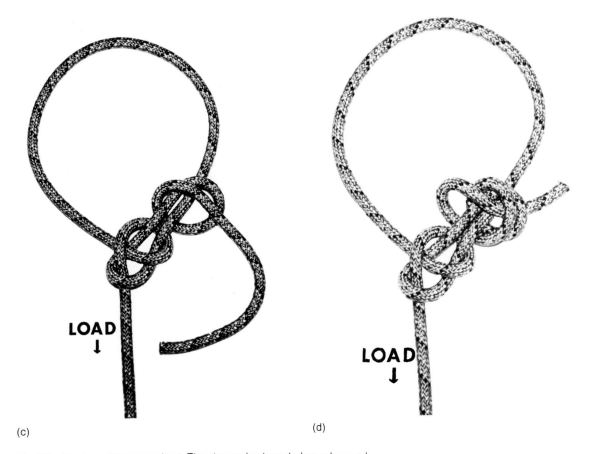

(c)   (d)

Fig 113   Bowline with stopper knot. The stopper knot must always be used.

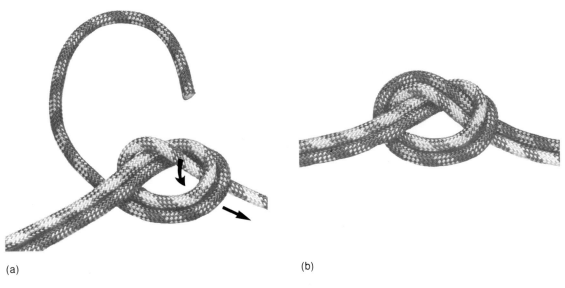

(a)   (b)

Fig 114   Tape knot.

(a)

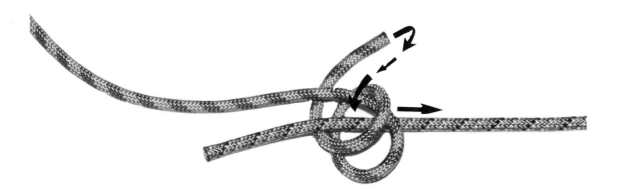

(b)

(c)

(d)

(e)

Fig 115   Double fisherman's knot.

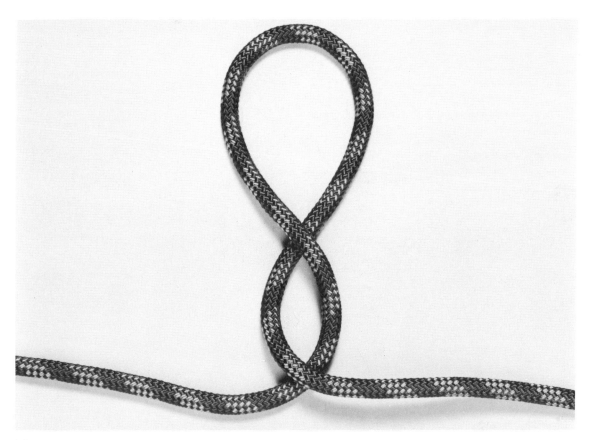

(a)

(b)

130

(c)

(d)

Fig 116   Alpine butterfly.

Tying On

The method illustrated in Figs 117 to 121 is suitable if you are only using a sit harness; if you intend to use a full body harness follow the individual manufacturer's instructions closely – each harness tends to vary in the method used. Figs 122 to 125 show the way to tie on to the middle of the rope.

The distance between each party member is critical and has implications when we consider crevasse rescue. Measuring the rope can be done in two ways. You can either measure how long each coil is around your chest as you tie on or you can measure the length of an arm-span and then uncoil the correct amount. Whichever method you use, practise it so you can accurately measure the rope to the nearest metre.

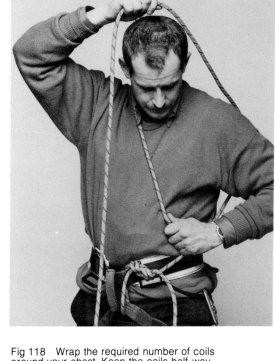

Fig 118 Wrap the required number of coils around your chest. Keep the coils half-way between your armpit and your waist.

Fig 117 Tying on; tie into the harness using the method recommended by the manufacturer. Here we are using a figure-of-eight knot tied by following the lay of the rope in a single figure-of-eight.

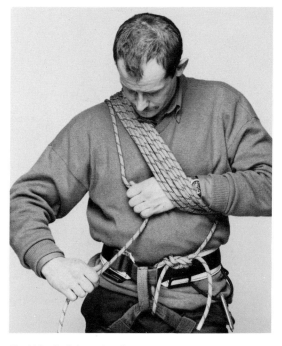

Fig 119 Pull through a loop.

Fig 120   Tie the loop around the rope in front of you with an overhand knot.

Fig 121   Clip the overhand knot into the karabiner and finally tie a figure-of-eight on the bight just under arm's reach away, this will enable you to hold the rope firmly.

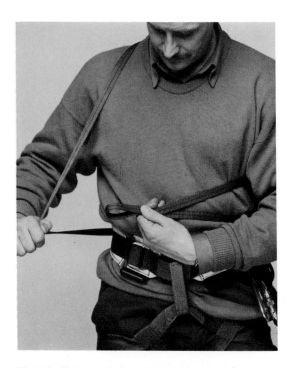

Fig 122   Tying on in the middle of the rope; make a chest harness with your sling. Pass your arm through one end and pull the other end around your back and underneath the other arm.

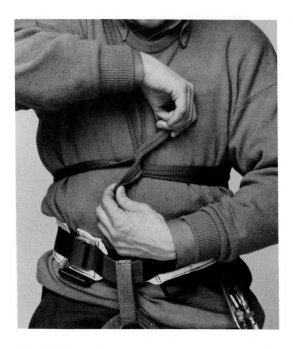

Fig 123   Tie the two ends together as shown and clip to the harness with a karabiner.

Fig 124

Fig 125

Fig 126 Use a long Alpine butterfly and a figure-of-eight on the bight to attach yourself to the rope. Having the knot extended in this way gives you more flexibility when skiing.

Prussiking

Prussiking is a method by which you can ascend the rope. There are a number of mechanical devices available but all add weight to what is already a heavy sack, so I will restrict myself to describing methods

that only use rope. Prussik rope should be 6mm or 7mm in diameter; the thicker it is, the stronger the sling becomes, but it is harder to make the thicker ropes grip. There are a great many variations of prussik knot, so I will only teach you those which I feel you will need. The diagrams are self-explanatory and the accompanying text describes the relative pros and cons of each knot. By experimenting you will be able to decide which you prefer using in any particular situation. I will use the term prussik to refer to all types of prussik knot.

Having learned the knots it is now time to look at the actual process of ascending the rope. You will need a prussik for your feet and one for your harness. I prefer the harness one to be short but others like it to be at arm's length; again, experiment and choose the system you find easiest. For our purposes put the foot prussik below the harness prussik, this will allow you to move the foot prussik with both hands. As you stand up in the foot loop try to move the harness prussik at the same time, this will save a lot of energy. Coming back down is just the reverse of going up. When you are fairly practised, you should try it carrying a heavy sack and wearing skis.

The first problem you will experience is

Two skiers

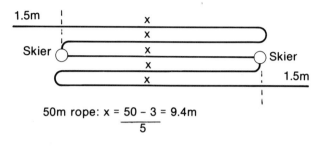

50m rope: x = $\frac{50 - 3}{5}$ = 9.4m

45m rope: x = $\frac{45 - 3}{5}$ = 8.4m (This is barely enough rope to be safe)

Proportioning the rope in this way allows each skier enough rope to drop to his partner. The extra 1.5m allows for the stretch in the rope.

Three skiers

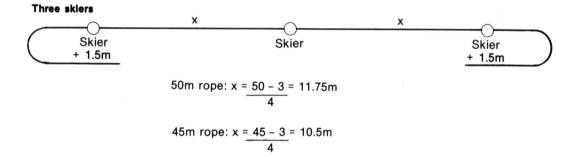

50m rope: x = $\frac{50 - 3}{4}$ = 11.75m

45m rope: x = $\frac{45 - 3}{4}$ = 10.5m

Four skiers

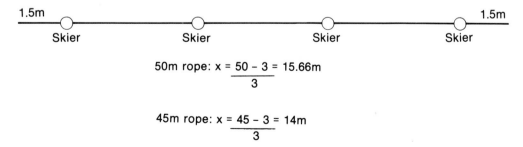

50m rope: x = $\frac{50 - 3}{3}$ = 15.66m

45m rope: x = $\frac{45 - 3}{3}$ = 14m

Fig 127   Proportioning the rope.

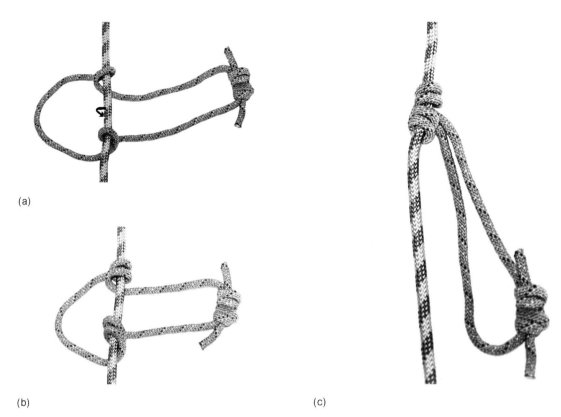

(a)

(b)   (c)

Fig 128   The classic prussik is easy to tie with one hand and works in both directions. If it slips, add another wrap.

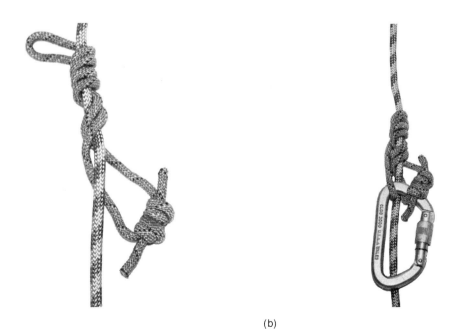

(a)   (b)

Fig 129   The French prussik (also known as the Marchand knot) works in both directions, and can be released under load by pulling down on top of the knot.

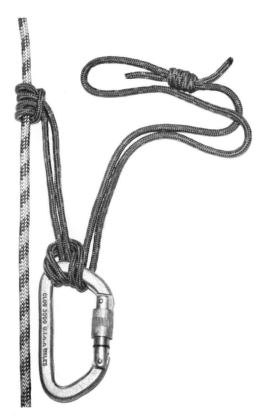

Fig 130   An alternative is to use a classic prussik and an Italian hitch tied off.

that the sack may tend to turn you upside-down, if so it will be necessary to remove it. It is generally preferable to remove it anyway as it makes the prussiking easier. Clip a karabiner to the rope and clip your poles into it, take the coils from around your shoulders, remove the sack and, using one of your long slings and a karabiner, attach the sack to the rope in front of you. Some people anticipate this by already having a piece of rope tied to their sacks. If you have tucked your ice-axe between your shoulders and the sack, take care not to drop it as you remove the sack. The next stage is to remove your skis, clipping each one in turn to this same karabiner. When you have taken off both skis tie them up as shown in Fig 138 and attach them to the karabiner, making sure the tips hang down so that they are easier to haul up. Everything is now ready for you to start prussiking.

The first few feet are the most difficult,

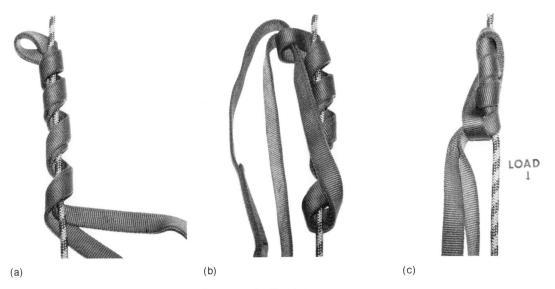

(a)   (b)   (c)

Fig 131   A modified French prussik (also known as the Klemheist). This will work with 1-inch tape or thicker rope.

137

Prussiking

Fig 132   Sitting in your harness hold the rope below and pull the foot prussik up towards you.

Fig 133   Stand up in the foot loop moving the chest prussik as you go.

Fig 134   Repeat the procedure. To descend reverse the process.

move only a few centimetres at a time and try to relax at each stage, do not fight it because you will only exhaust yourself. If it is proving to be very difficult you are probably doing something wrong: stop and rethink. Prussiking is always awkward, but you can reduce the effort needed considerably by organising yourself well. You should practise until you are confident that you can extricate yourself from the end of a rope without any assistance.

Belaying

Belaying is the act of controlling the rope so that you can hold a fall. It is absolutely vital that you are tight on your anchors and have anticipated the direction of the fall so that you will not be jerked on to the anchor, which would stress it more than is necessary. I have illustrated two methods:

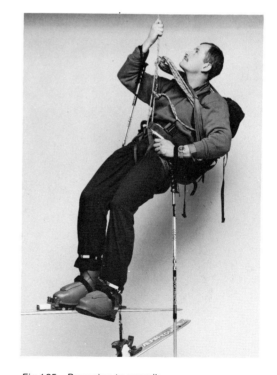

Fig 135   Preparing to prussik.

Fig 136 First clip your poles to the rope using a karabiner. Remove your sack and slings if the sack is going to stop you from prussiking or is tending to turn you over (if you have tied on correctly this should not happen). Clip the sack via a sling to the same karabiner as the poles.

Fig 137 Remove the skis very carefully and attach them to the karabiner with the tips down (this will help to prevent them catching as you pull them out).

Fig 138 The method of tying the skis together. Wrap the sling around the skis, passing it back through itself. Finish with a half-hitch. At some stage the sling should pass through the binding to ensure absolute security.

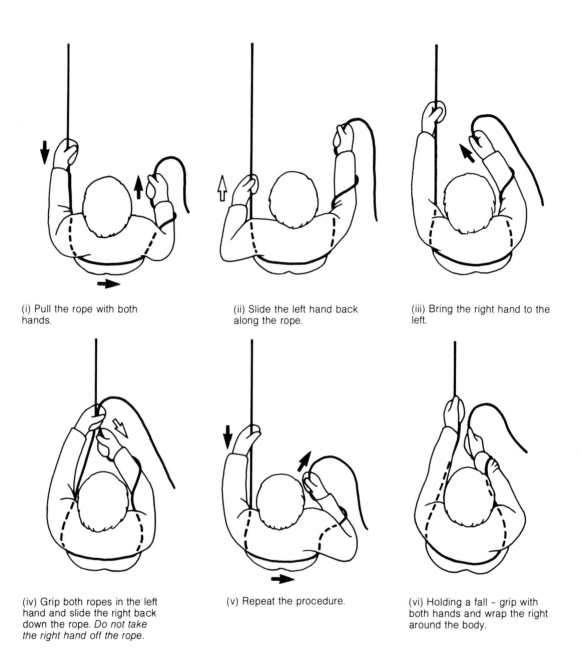

(i) Pull the rope with both hands.

(ii) Slide the left hand back along the rope.

(iii) Bring the right hand to the left.

(iv) Grip both ropes in the left hand and slide the right back down the rope. *Do not take the right hand off the rope.*

(v) Repeat the procedure.

(vi) Holding a fall – grip with both hands and wrap the right around the body.

➡ Hand moves rope

⇨ Hand slides over rope

Fig 139   The waist belay.

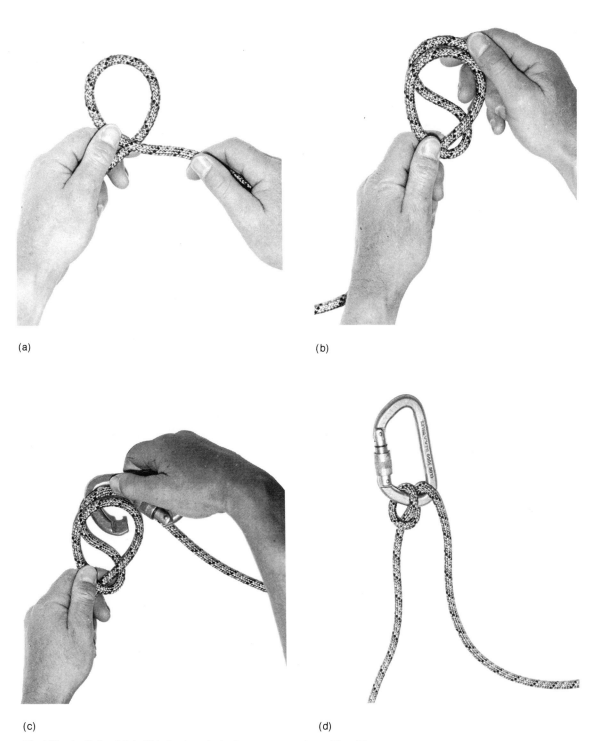

(a)

(b)

(c)

(d)

Fig 140   An Italian hitch. This knot works better on a pear-shaped karabiner.

Fig 141   Italian hitch locked off, using two half-hitches on a bight of the rope.

the waist belay and the Italian hitch. Use the waist belay when the rope is frozen or the anchor is suspect, otherwise the Italian hitch is usually preferable.

Anchoring

This is the process by which we tie ourselves securely to the mountainside. There are many methods available to the mountaineer, but I will restrict myself to those which are most relevant to the tourer. The only occasions that we are likely to need anchors are when we have to test-ski a suspect slope or extricate someone from a crevasse. With this in mind, the following methods should prove more than adequate. However, they all rely on a certain amount of judgement and should be practised in safety first and preferably under the watchful eye of an experienced friend or Guide. If we belay directly on to the anchor point it is known as a direct belay; if we tie ourselves to the anchor and then belay on to our body it is known as an indirect belay.

Rock anchors come in three forms: spikes, chockstones and jammed knots. Spikes can either be used to anchor to or they can be used to provide a direct belay. To anchor to them simply make a loop with a figure-of-eight knot and pass it over the spike – be sure that the rope will not slip off. An alternative which you would use to adjust your position is to pass the rope around the spike, clipping it back to yourself with a pear-shaped karabiner and a clove hitch (Figs 142 & 143). There are two ways you can use a direct belay; the first is to put a sling around the spike, clip a pear-shaped karabiner to it and use the Italian hitch. The second method is to run the rope around the spike, keeping it tight as the skier descends. Ensure that the rope does not run over a sharp edge in the process. This method relies on the friction between the rock and the rope.

To anchor to a chockstone, which is a boulder jammed in a crack, it is necessary to pass the rope behind the chockstone and then attach it to yourself in the normal way with a clove hitch. If there are no chockstones or spikes look for a flared crack, tie a figure-of-eight knot and jam it into the crack. Needless to say, with all of these anchors solid rock must be used.

If there is no rock to anchor to you will have to use the snow. The simplest anchor is to sit in the snow, dig the tails of your skis in and use a waist belay or Italian hitch off your harness. A variation of this is to pass a sling around the skis between the snow and your boots and for a partner to use an Italian hitch from the sling.

If a more solid anchor is required you

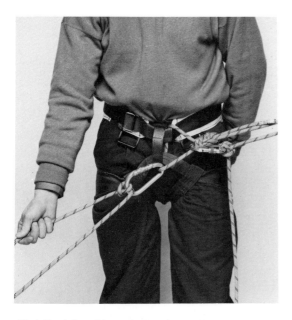

Fig 142 Adjustable anchoring; the rope goes from the harness to the anchor and then back to the harness where it is fixed via a karabiner and clove hitch. The Italian hitch is then fastened to the tie-in loop.

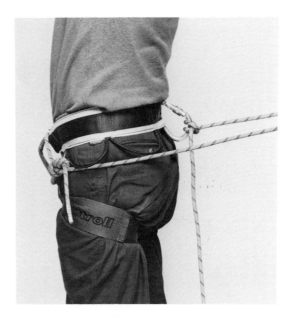

Fig 143 If you are using a waist belay you must clip the karabiner to the rear of your harness; this will prevent any rotation of your body which in turn could cause you to drop the rope.

Fig 144 Direct belaying with an Italian hitch.

Fig 145 Direct belaying around a spike.

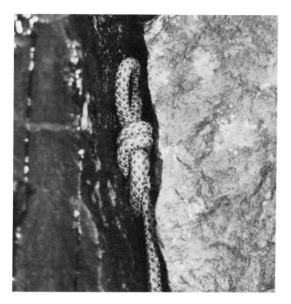

Fig 146 A jammed knot.

can use a buried axe or buried ski system. The depth at which you bury it will depend on the snow: the softer the snow, the deeper you bury the axe or ski. The angle of the trough is very important to ensure that when the system is loaded the axe or ski is pulled even deeper. It is equally important to make the exit trough for the rope deep enough, otherwise when the rope is loaded it will lift the axe or ski up and out. It is usual to attach a sling around the balance point of the axe using a clove hitch and then to belay to that. If you are using skis turn them tip to tail so that the binding mounting screws are off-set and then proceed as with the axe. This is one

Fig 147 Anchoring on a partner. A sling is passed around the skier's skis behind his boots and the skis are jammed into the snow. A hollow is cut into the snow for the skier to sit into.

144

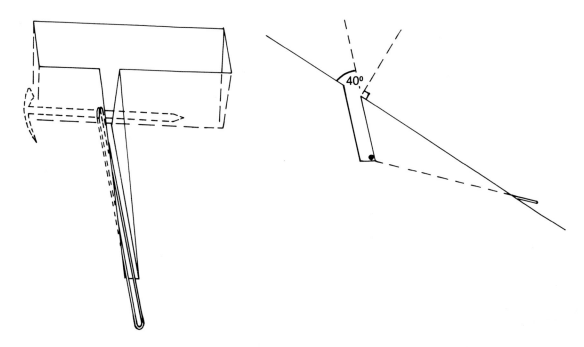

Fig 148 The buried axe belay. The angle of 40 degrees is fairly critical, so stick a ski pole in at 90 degrees to the surface (this is easier to judge), halve it (45 degrees) and then dig the trench a few degrees further back. Position your body below the exit point of the sling and if the snow is at all soft use a waist belay.

of the most useful anchoring systems because, if correctly constructed, it is quick, simple and safe.

The final system I will show you is what is known as a snow mushroom or bollard, which is cut with the ice-axe. In very soft snow line the back of the trench with your ski poles or rucksacks. The bollard must be overhanging so that the rope cannot slip off; its size depends upon the state of the snow – the softer the snow the bigger the bollard. In very soft conditions it may have a diameter of two metres (two yards) coming down to one metre in harder more compact snows. Be careful if the snow-pack shows signs of layering, as the rope can then cut in thus lifting the layers above clean away.

I must reiterate that all anchors rely on a great deal of subjective judgement, and only experience and testing lots of different types will allow you to construct them with any degree of confidence.

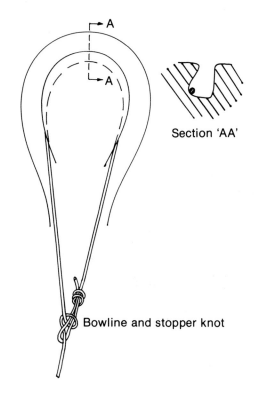

Section 'AA'

Bowline and stopper knot

Fig 149 The snow mushroom/bollard.

145

Crevasse Rescue

Apart from test-skiing suspect slopes, the only other occasion on which you are likely to need the rope is when you are skiing crevassed terrain. Glaciers are made of ice which is a plastic material and which when bent excessively will crack. This bending will occur whenever the ice flows over a convex slope, and so cracks or crevasses will appear. A popular myth is that crevasses will suddenly open up, swallow the skier and then close again, taking the victim with it. This does not occur; although a glacier is constantly moving, it moves very slowly, and it is the snow covering the crevasse that suddenly gives way. It is important to realise this, because late in the day, after the snow has melted in the sun, these snow bridges will not be as strong. This is one of the reasons

that climbers start climbing in the hours of darkness so that they can finish the route before the sun has had a chance to soften the snow bridges. If you have to cross crevassed terrain, regardless of the time of day, you should rope up.

Ascending presents little difficulty since the party will move together at roughly the same pace and if someone does fall into a crevasse it will be easy to hold them, because there will normally be at least one party member still below the crevasse. It is unlikely that the last member will fall in where the others have passed, although it is not unheard of. Also, because you are on skins and travelling slowly it should be easier to hold a fall.

Skiing down through crevassed terrain is more hazardous because you will be travelling faster and will have to ski roped together. Skiing roped together takes a

Fig 150 Practising skiing roped together on a quiet piste. Notice the position of the hand loop.

Fig 151 Beware of crevasses. An Aspirant Guide from the Ecole Nationale de Ski et Alpinism in Chamonix practising crevasse rescue realistically.

Fig 152 Crevasse rescue. Notice the rope cutting in on the left and the lined channel that has been dug out.

great deal of practice and teamwork and should be practised either on a quiet piste or on a safe off-piste run. No matter how good you are, ski slowly and in control. I find that stem turns are the most suitable to use. With one hand on the figure-of-eight hand loop, I use a pole in the other to help lift the rope out of the way. For reasons that I will explain shortly, your ice-axe must be easily accessible.

If someone does fall through you must act very quickly and skid to a halt, falling into the snow in the opposite direction to the crevasse and at the same time keeping a firm grip on the loop. If this sounds improbable, perhaps the following story will give you some confidence.

When I visited ENSA to observe the

French training their Guides, we set off down the Vallée Blanche to find somewhere to practise crevasse rescue. My own experience to that date was purely theoretical; the only falls I had been involved in were not serious, with the victims stopping at their armpits. When we reached a suitably crevassed section our professor turned to us and in his broken English said 'OK, now we practise crevasse rescue. Martyn, you ski into this crevasse, your friend will hold you.' As the colour visibly drained from my face a wry grin developed on his: 'OK your partner [a young Aspirant French Guide] will ski and you will hold the fall.' Before I had time to protest my inexperience, Jacques was off. As he shot over the edge into the crevasse I skidded to a halt and waited for the jerk. I could feel Jacques, but the pull was not nearly as bad as I thought it would be. Our professor naturally knew what he was doing. The only types of crevasse we are likely to fall into are the unseen ones that are covered by a soft snow bridge. As the snow bridge collapses and you fall through, the rope will start to cut into the soft snow, and much of the force of the fall is absorbed by this action. Some people even recommend tying figure-of-eight knots at about two metre (two yard) intervals along the rope to aid this process. The drawback of this is that it shortens the rope considerably, even though it does make it easier to hold a fall. The crevasse rescue strategy that I am about to describe assumes such soft snow conditions.

Stage One

Hold the fall. The victim will remove his sack and skis, taking great care not to drop them, and fasten them to the rope in the manner described in the prussiking section.

Stage Two

Establish communications with the victim. If there are more than two of you this is

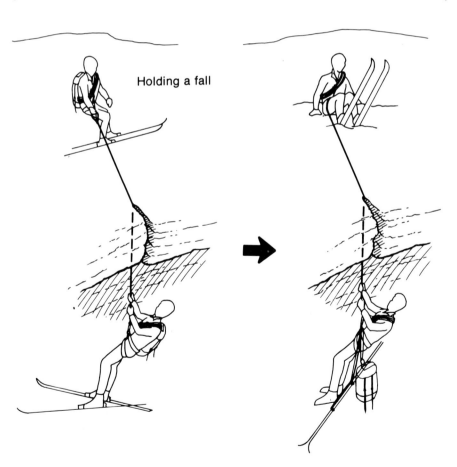

Holding a fall

Fig 153 Crevasse rescue: stage 1.

easy because the other members, protected by the rope, can move to a vantage point. If, however, there are only two of you, proceed to Stage Three first.

Stage Three

Construct an anchor. First dig the heels of your skis into the snow as this will make you feel more secure. Then, using your axe (hence the need for it to be accessible), make a buried axe anchor. You should be able to let go with the hand that is holding the rope and let the weight come on to your harness, freeing both hands to make the anchor. Attach the anchor to the rope below the hand loop using a long sling and a French prussik, or a normal prussik and an Italian hitch. Escape from the rope and back this up with a locked off Italian hitch on the rope clipped into the anchor (this is all so that the system can be released). The hitch must be locked off so that the *slack* rope can take a load. If you are on your own you can now establish communications, ensuring your own safety at the same time.

Stage Four

Rescue the victim. You must now consider the following options and I suggest you

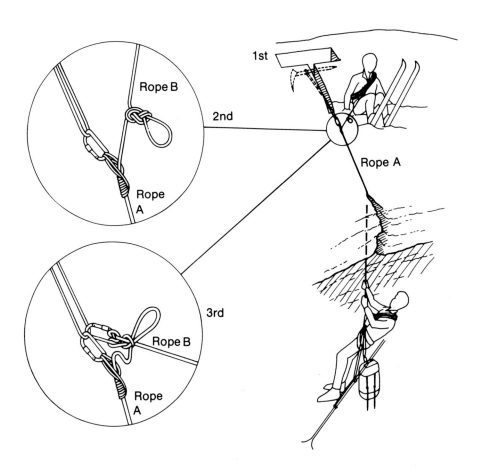

Fig 154 Crevasse rescue: stage 3. Lock off the Italian hitch so that rope B can take a load.

Fig 155   The splendour of the Alps.

Fig 156   Martin Burrows-Smith on Crotched Gulley in the Cairngorms, Scotland.

150

Fig 157   In Morocco you can get a lift half-way.

always look at them in this order.

1. Can he climb out? If so, release the system and protect him with the rope. It may even be desirable to lower him down to a snow bridge that would then allow him to climb out.
2. Are there sufficient people on the surface to be able to literally haul the victim out? If so, proceed to Stage Five.
3. Can the victim prussik out?
4. If none of the above are possible you will have to set up a hauling system, so proceed to Stage Five.

Stage Five

Clear the snow from the edge of the crevasse for one metre's (one yard's) width to one side of where the rope has cut in. Be careful not to knock too much debris on to the victim. This trough should be lined with ski poles, skis or a sack to prevent the rope cutting in. Make sure that

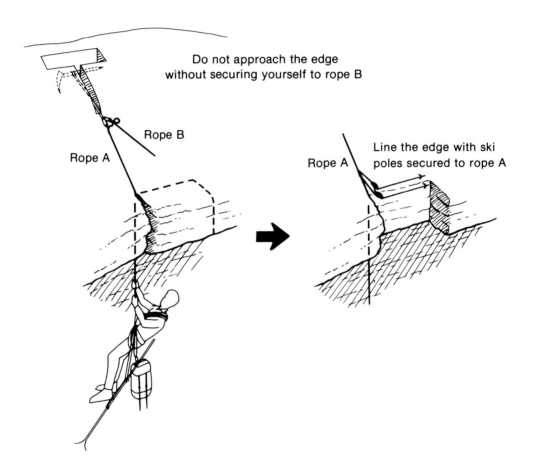

Do not approach the edge
without securing yourself to rope B

Rope B

Rope A

Rope A

Line the edge with ski
poles secured to rope A

Fig 158 Crevasse rescue: stage 5. The following procedure assumes there are only two of you which is the worst situation in which you should find yourself. If the victim is unable to assist in any way proceed to stage 6 and prussik or abseil (a method that is well known to mountaineers but not usually needed by tourers) down, fix the loop of rope in position, administer first aid, prussik back up and continue as described.

whatever you use is secure and will not disappear down the hole. It may be possible to free the entrapped rope and lift it on to this padding, but it is unlikely. If the victim is prussiking out this trough will help considerably, although it might be necessary to drop a spare bit of rope for him to transfer to when he reaches the buried part of his rope. The victim should try to free this as he prussiks by it. If you are left with no alternative but to haul, proceed to Stage Six.

Stage Six

Tie a figure-of-eight one metre (one yard) from the locked off Italian hitch, or use

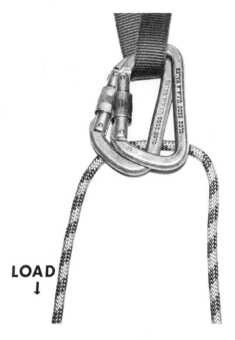

Fig 160   Garda knot; although there is an increase in friction there will be no slippage, so it is a good system to use in a confined situation. Both karabiners must be exactly the same.

Fig 159   Clutches; pulley and French prussik. This is the most efficient because of the use of the pulley, but the prussik must be just the right length to prevent any slippage back through the system.

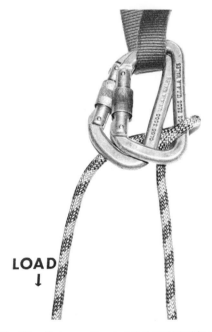

Fig 161   First pass the rope that you want to slip through one karabiner (see Fig 162).

153

LOAD
↓

Fig 162   Then pass the rope that will take the load through two karabiners.

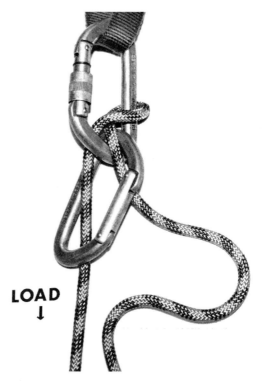

LOAD
↓

Fig 164   Stufleffer hitch.

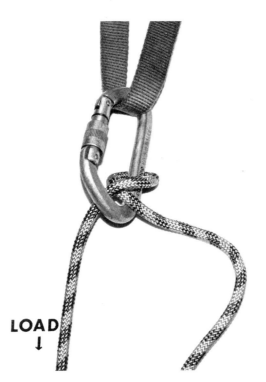

LOAD
↓

Fig 163   Stufleffer hitch; this works in the same way as the Garda knot but will work with two dissimilar karabiners.

the hand loop if it is in a suitable position and attach a clutch system to this same figure-of-eight.

Stage Seven

Using the remaining rope (there should be enough if you have tied on at the correct intervals), drop a loop to the victim who, using his pulley, can clip into this loop and attach the pulley to his harness. If the loop is not long enough you can extend it by clipping your spare sling to it, using your own pulley between the loop and the sling. The victim then clips into the sling. Fix the spare rope left in your hand to the clutch.

Stage Eight

Fasten a French prussik to the rope going down to the victim from the clutch and with a karabiner clip the spare rope

154

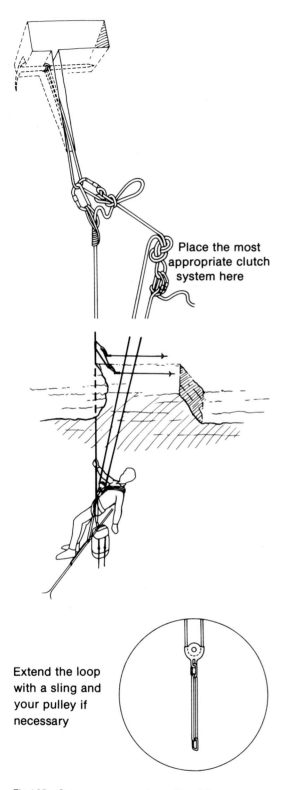

Place the most appropriate clutch system here

Extend the loop with a sling and your pulley if necessary

Fig 165 Crevasse rescue: stages 6 and 7.

through this. If you now pull on this spare rope you will have a hoisting system. As the French prussik nears the clutch release the rope, allow the clutch to work and move the French prussik back down to the edge. Then repeat the process all over again until the rescue has been completed. The victim can help by pulling on the entrapped rope, which he should try to free as he approaches it. Once free, the victim is very likely to be suffering from hypothermia and will need to be treated appropriately (*see* appendix).

I have seen and experimented with many different systems, but this is the simplest and most applicable to our situation. Many of the others do not take into account the fact that the rope will almost certainly be trapped in the snow. If the rope is not trapped and will run easily, use a clutch instead of the locked off Italian hitch. Undo the hand loop and proceed as before, missing out the French prussik. This time the victim can help much more by pulling on the rope that links the pulley to the clutch. This is known as an assisted hoist and is extremely efficient.

You must be prepared to improvise in all rescue situations and you must therefore practise them in safety. I would not recommend that you practise them in the same way the Aspirant Guides did; they were experienced and were being supervised by some of the most knowledgeable instructors around. Fortunately, much effective practice can be undertaken away from the snow. However, a friend of mine once had great difficulty convincing a police officer that he was not about to hang himself when he decided to practise in the trees of a local park. Eventually you should try on real snow, but do so under the guidance of somebody with more

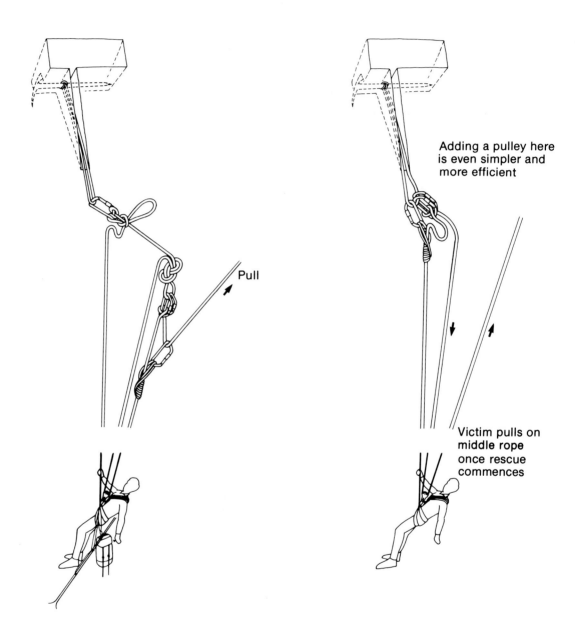

Pull

Adding a pulley here
is even simpler and
more efficient

Victim pulls on
middle rope
once rescue
commences

Fig 166 Crevasse rescue: stage 8. The ropes
have been spread out for clarity.

Fig 167   Crevasse rescue: the assisted hoist.

experience than yourself and make sure that every stage is backed up in case you make a mistake.

Navigation

The ability to navigate accurately in winter conditions, whether it be across the Cairngorm plateau in Scotland, the Haute route in the Alps or even in more remote regions such as the Atlas mountains or the high Himalayas, is essential in order to operate in reasonable safety. Fortunately, good maps and accurate guidebooks are available to most areas, but these are of no use unless the tourer can use them precisely. It is beyond the realms of this book to teach you navigation, but I have included some useful reference material in the bibliography. I will assume that you have mastered the basic techniques and so I will show you how to adapt your knowledge to the touring situation.

Interpreting the Map

The first basic skill must be the ability to interpret the features on the map and in particular the contours. Remember that a lot of snow will often soften the landscape, effectively hiding many of the smaller features that you might normally recognise. Allow for this when you are trying to imagine what a feature should look like. Use the contours to anticipate where there might be avalanche danger and plan your route accordingly. Steep slopes with the contours close together will be more dangerous than shallower slopes. I cannot give you definitive advice here because there are too many factors involved, but an awareness is half the battle.

Assessing Distance

The second basic skill is the ability to assess distance on the map and this is perhaps the hardest thing for the tourer to do. Going uphill is not too difficult as you can apply the same techniques of timing as for walking. Again, definitive figures like 4 k.p.h. (2½ m.p.h.) are fairly meaningless, because it will depend upon the condition of the snow, the direction of the wind, the fitness of the party, and so on. What you must do is try to develop a sense of your pace: how fast are you going when you can breathe with ease? How fast when you start feeling out of breath and how fast when you are panting? Remember to allow for acclimatisation if you are just starting a tour.

Going downhill is much harder because we all ski at different speeds, and this is when our altimeter is invaluable. Providing we have been able to set it up at a known height within the last half-hour to an hour, it should still be fairly accurate. Let's say that we want to cross a glacier at a given point in order to avoid an ice fall lower down. Look at the contours and find out the height of the crossing point, then all you have to do is to ski down until your altimeter reads that height and you should be approximately there.

Compass

I have left compass work to the end because many people rely on it too much. In the high mountains, be aware that the mountains themselves can be magnetic and can give false readings. Some transceivers can also deflect the needle if the compass is held too close. When you are in a white-out, however, you will have to rely on the compass to orientate yourself, so make sure you are well practised in its use in these conditions.

If you cannot navigate take the trouble to learn; not only does it make you safer, but it can be great fun. The aforementioned hints will help you to make the transition to the mountains where the ability to know where you are and where you are going will enhance the whole experience.

EQUIPMENT CHECKLIST

Individual

skis
poles
spare basket
skins
harschisen
spare skin glue
rag
wax
two elastic bands (in case heel of
 skin does not stick)
needle and thread (for skin
 repairs)
binding spares (replacement
 screws etc. for parts that
 may come undone) and tools
boots
spare boot clips
crampons
ice-axe
personal clothing
spare socks (can double as
 spare gloves in an
 emergency)
spare jumper
spare hat, gloves/mittens
sun-glasses
goggles
sun cream
transceiver

spare batteries
harness
four 2,500kg screwgate
 karabiners (including one
 pear-shaped karabiner)
two 8 foot 1 inch tape slings
 (approximate length
 of tape)
pulley
two prussik loops
water bottle
food
first-aid kit
survival bag
compass
map
guidebook
altimeter
head torch
spare batteries
spare bulb
rucksack

Party Equipment

rope
at least two shovels
stretcher
inflatable splint (desirable
 but not essential)
emergency sleeping bag
major injuries first-aid kit
cooking equipment

Huts

Throughout the mountainous areas of the world you will find huts. These vary between plain wooden shacks and quite luxurious buildings that are almost hotels. Some are manned, some provide food, others just a roof. Their use enables the tourer to carry a much smaller sack and to stay up in the mountains for a longer period. They are, however, popular and can get very crowded. Each country has a slightly different system within their huts so before embarking upon a tour check with the local tourist office or Guides' Bureau as to the availability of beds and the facilities that exist. The huts are maintained in general by the mountaineering association of the host nation. If you are a member of such a body, then reciprocal rights do exist which will help to reduce the costs.

Emergency Procedures

Unfortunately anybody can get caught out no matter how well prepared they might be; the preparations merely reduce the possibilities of an accident, they cannot eliminate them altogether.

Fig 168   A snow hole. The entrance has been sheltered by the use of blocks.

Fig 169   Inside a snow hole. A mat is used to insulate the body from the snow and the walls have been smoothed to prevent drips.

Stretchers

Every touring party should carry an emergency stretcher system. These usually involve using the skis as runners, linked together with some form of canvas or nylon bed. They all vary so look carefully at the manufacturer's instructions regarding their construction and link everything together with the rope. Normally it will take at least three people to handle the stretcher, one at the front and two behind (Fig 170).

Skiing down with one of these light, flimsy stretchers is hard work because you must always ski fairly slowly – the stretcher cannot stand being bounced around like the blood wagons they use on-piste. It will often, however, be much quicker to get an injured person off the mountain this way than to send for help. If you have sent for help be sure to make yourselves as visible as possible, using the survival bags or anything else that is brightly coloured to mark your position, and then shelter yourselves while you wait for the rescuers to arrive.

Building a Shelter

If you are benighted you will have to find or build a shelter: to stay out in the open is to court disaster. You should have a shovel or two in the party, so find a deep bank of snow and dig horizontally into it. The smaller the hole the better, as it will then be easier to close up. If you don't have any shovels, use the tails of your skis to cut blocks away; your ice-axe can also be used and you can buy snow saws designed specifically for this purpose. Digging is hard, sweaty work so strip off to prevent your clothing from becoming soaked, which will become very uncomfortable later.

When you have got about two metres (two yards) in, start to dig at right-angles to this first tunnel. If there is more than

Fig 170 Skiing with a stretcher.

one of you digging, you can either dig in the opposite direction creating a T-shaped hole or the other person could start at the same time digging an L-shaped hole to join up with yours. Once inside, you can enlarge the hole as much as you like; keep the walls and ceiling as smooth as possible to prevent corners that will allow drips to

form (the temperature will normally be just above freezing) and dig a small trough so that the cold air can sink below the level at which you are sleeping. It is vital to have an air hole and if you are experiencing headaches it could be that there is insufficient through-draught of fresh air. Take a shovel inside with you so that if the hole

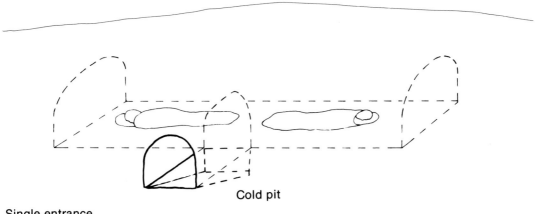

Cold pit

Single entrance

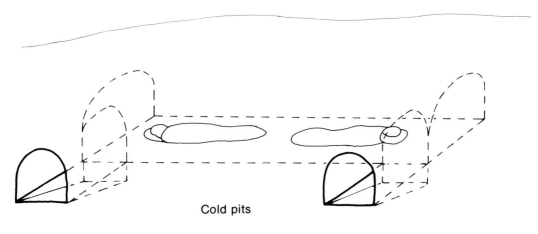

Cold pits

Double entrance

Fig 171 Snow holes.

does collapse for any reason you can dig yourself out. The outside should be clearly marked so that anybody who leaves the snow hole can easily find it again. In white-out conditions it is a good idea to attach a rope to the snow hole and anyone then leaving can keep hold of the rope. Snow holes are a real life-saver and the shelter they offer is invaluable.

There are many alternatives to this basic snow hole: you can build out using the blocks you have cut free, possibly reducing the amount of digging in the process, but to build a complete igloo is, in my experience, too time-consuming and rarely necessary. If the snow is not deep enough for a hole this might be the only alternative, although it is usually possible to employ the skis and your survival bags to good effect to at least close in the roof, thereby reducing the amount of work. If the snow is all powder and you cannot find a deep enough hollow, build a large mound, keep adding to it and eventually it will consolidate enough for you to dig into it and to hollow it out, creating a type of igloo. This does, however, take a long time.

The decision of whether to try to get down or to dig in is always difficult and there are too many factors to be able to give clear advice, but once you have decided to dig in and create a shelter make the best one possible and look after

yourself, taking extra care to keep warm and dry. Work on a 'buddy system' of everybody helping to look after each other. Remember to insulate yourself from the ground and undo any tight clothing, especially your boots as this will help your circulation and therefore keep you warmer. Protect your head from the cold, and if your extremities get really cold stick them into your groin or, if it is your feet, someone else's groin; under your armpits is another good warm spot. The old ideas of rubbing with snow or drinking alcohol are now definitely out (*see* appendix).

I hope that you will never be caught in such conditions, but if you are remember that survival is more a state of mind than anything else, and hopefully the above hints will prove useful. Many people actually use snow-holing as a daily means of shelter instead of tents when touring in remote areas, and it can in fact be quite an enjoyable experience.

The skills of ski touring can open up vast areas of mountains for both skiing and exploring; they demand a lot from you but the rewards are usually worth the effort and commitment. I wish you all good skiing at whatever level you participate; treat the mountains with the respect they deserve and I am sure you will grow old happily with many good memories.

Appendix

First Aid

First aid normally implies just that – the very first aid that you give to an injured person. This is perfectly adequate to cope with accidents in the normal environment where professional help is close at hand, but in the mountains that help may be hours or, in the case of a remote tour, days away. Because of this you owe it to yourself and those with you to gain further knowledge of this subject. In this appendix I will only be able to outline the areas where you should expand your knowledge; to try to do more than this would require another book. I have included some further reading suggestions in the bibliography.

However gory the accident, your first priority must be your own safety and that of your party. Do not rush in; it is better to take a couple of deep breaths and to prepare yourself for the worst. Everybody suffers some form of shock when confronted by a nasty accident, you should expect it and that will help you to cope with it. Approach the casualty with an air of confidence, even if you do not feel confident. Your manner will have a tremendous effect on them; do not underestimate this factor.

The first thing you should check, regardless of any blood and other obvious injuries, is that the casualty is breathing and that his airway is clear. If it is not, proceed with artificial respiration immediately, checking at the same time to see if he has a pulse. If there is no discernible pulse, perform external cardiac massage simultaneously with EAR (expired air resuscitation). This type of injury is quite common in avalanche victims so it is an important technique to learn and in fact is really quite easy.

Once the victim is breathing you should check the whole of the body to see the extent of any other injuries. Do not go straight for the obvious ones, because you may well miss something more serious. Talk to your patient and build up a relationship with him, he is now your responsibility until you can hand over to someone of greater authority like a doctor. Do not be concerned about this responsibility, however, you are very unlikely to do any harm and will probably, even with only little knowledge, do a great deal of good.

Any wounds should be closed up using either dressings from your first-aid kit or by direct pressure with your hands.

Fractures and dislocations should be immobilised in the position of most comfort and strapped up very firmly, especially if you plan to move the casualty. It is really quite simple; you must always ask yourself whether if you do not do something the condition will worsen so you might as well try, particularly in the case of breathing and the heart. If you do not try then the casualty will die anyway! There are many first-aid courses available; if you do not have the above knowledge then perhaps you should take one – they are useful for everyday life as well.

With all injuries there will be associated shock in the victim. This is a serious condition, especially in a hostile environment, and yet it is easy to treat. Talking to him will have helped enormously, but you should now keep the patient warm. Hot drinks may be appropriate if the patient is unlikely to get to the hospital for a number of hours, but not if sooner because it will interfere with any anaesthetics that might need to be given. Food should be avoided for the same reasons.

I know this is brief, but the intention is to get you to seek further expert training. I will now mention some of the problems that are more specific to our situation. The cold can be a hazard in several ways. Hypothermia occurs when the body's temperature drops. It is a progressive condition: people behave irrationally, start falling over a lot, shiver, fumble and their eyesight becomes blurred. The sooner you realise a party member is suffering from hypothermia the better, he will not recognise it himself. Stop, put on warm clothing and find shelter. Administer food and hot drinks and if the casualty revives you can continue down (not on with the trip), keeping a close eye on him to make sure he does not deteriorate again. If he does, repeat the procedure again. If he does not recover, you will have to consolidate your shelter and send for assistance.

More local cold injuries are frost-nip and frost-bite. Frost-nip is the first stage of frost-bite and will appear as a blanching of the skin, often unnoticed by the patient. It commonly occurs in the extremities and in the cheeks, earlobes, nose and forehead. Rewarm the affected area immediately and protect it more efficiently from the cold. With facial instances you can hold your hands up to your face and breathe warm air over the affected parts; the colour should rapidly return. If it does not, the patient probably has frost-bite and in this case you should not attempt to rewarm the affected part but return as quickly as possible to medical help. Whilst the limb is frozen it will be possible for the victim to continue to use it, thereby speeding up the evacuation.

Just as serious as cold-related injuries are those associated with the strength of the sun. Sunburn can be a serious problem for the uninitiated, but I hope all of you are sufficiently experienced to avoid it. If you are a newcomer to the high mountains be aware that the sun can be very strong and that it is made worse by the way in which it is reflected up from the snow. Protect yourself with a high factor sun cream and make sure you cover the areas under the chin, and nose which receive reflected light. The eyes must be protected at all times as the ultraviolet rays are very strong and the snow-blindness that results is very debilitating. Heat-stroke and dehydration can easily occur on tours: dress appropriately and drink plenty of water.

If you go touring you will be working hard continuously at altitude and your body will need to acclimatise so that it can work in this rarified atmosphere. There is less oxygen in the air so the blood has to produce more red blood cells to be able to absorb as much oxygen as possible. This has the effect of thickening the blood and if you have become dehydrated it will exasperate the problem, because dehydration also makes the heart work harder. The end result will be mountain sickness which can be very unpleasant. The way to avoid it is to go up slowly, if possible spending several days going over 3,000 metres (10,000 feet) and returning to the valley to sleep before staying up for a period. Be sure to drink plenty; if your urine is bright yellow it is a good sign that you are dehydrated. Acclimatisation is a strange thing because it is unrelated to fitness: one year you may suffer very little, whilst the next you may be very bad. Despite much research we still do not fully understand the process.

Glossary

ABMG Association of British Mountain Guides.

Anchoring Securing yourself to the mountainside.

Angulation Usually used to refer to the way in which the hips are dropped to the inside of a turn (hip angulation) and to the medial movement of the knees as a fine tuning movement (knee angulation).

Anticipation A preparatory rotation of the upper body in the direction of the new turn.

Avalement A French term meaning swallowing. Very similar to compression turns.

Ballistic As in stretching. A bouncing stretch, to be avoided because of the very real possibility of damaging tendons and muscle fibres.

Banking Leaning to the centre of the turn.

BASI British Association of Ski Instructors.

Basic swing A progression from ploughing to parallel turns.

Basket Usually a plastic ring on the bottom of the pole to prevent the pole from sinking in too far.

Belaying The action of controlling the rope so that a fall can be held.

Boiler plate A hard icy snow.

Bowline A knot used to tie around an object.

Buried axe/ski A form of anchor.

Button-lift A type of ski lift also known as a Poma.

Canting Methods which compensate for the variations in leg angles.

Check A sudden edging action which provides a platform.

Chockstone A boulder jammed in a crack.

Clo A measurement of the thermal resistance of clothing (its insulative value).

Clove hitch A knot used to anchor to a spar.

Clutch A system which allows the rope to run one way but not the other.

Compression turns A versatile method of turning that involves flexing the legs.

Corn snow Same as spring snow.

Cornice An overhanging crest of snow formed on the lee side of a ridge by the wind.

Crampons Spikes worn on boots to help grip the ice.

Crevasse A crack in the glacier caused by the ice flowing over a convex slope.

Cross-country A form of skiing using lighter equipment and different techniques.

Crud Bad snow.

Crust A hard surface to the snow that will sometimes but not always support the skier (breakable).

Depth hoar Fragile crystals formed within the snowpack.

Drag A lift which pulls skiers uphill on their skis.

Edging Angling the skis so that the metal edges can bite into the snow.

Fall-line The line a ball would take if

167

rolling freely down a hill.

Flow-line A line around which you feel yourself flow, more of a sensation than a clearly defined line.

Fracture line The line at which an avalanche has broken away.

Garda knot A form of clutch using two karabiners.

Graupel Hailstone-like snow.

Guide A qualified mountain guide who has a UIAGM carnet.

Hard pack Hard icy snow.

Harschisen Ski crampons.

Haute route A famous tour from Chamonix to Zermatt.

Heli-skiing Using the helicopter to lift you high into the mountains.

Hypothermia A lowering of the core temperature of the body.

Ice-axe A tool used by climbers and tourers for a variety of functions.

Imaging Another term for visualising.

Italian hitch A knot used in belaying.

Karabiner An aluminium snaplink made for climbing.

Kernmantle A type of rope.

Kick turn A way of changing direction whilst remaining in one spot.

Kinaesthetic Awareness of movement and motion.

Klemheist Another name for the modified French prussik.

Langlauf Cross-country skiing.

Marchand knot An alternative name for the French prussik.

Metamorphosis A process of change within the snowpack.

Mid stance A style of skiing which uses minimum extension and retraction of the legs and maintains a balanced position over the middle of the ski.

Modified French A form of prussik knot.

Mogul A bump of snow formed by the actions of skiers.

Névé Hard, old, firm snow.

Off-piste Any ungroomed slope.

Open stance Feet hip-width apart.

Piste Prepared ski run or track.

Pisteur Ski patroller.

Ploughing Skiing with the tips of the skis together and the tails apart.

Poma Form of drag lift.

Porridge Heavy wet snow.

Powder Light dry snow.

Prussik A knot that tightens up around another rope and will not slide.

Real snow Snow untouched by piste machines and other skiers, natural snow.

Rime ice Ice that forms on the lee side of objects and indicates the direction of the wind.

Safety strap A strap which joins your ski to your ankle so that you do not lose it in the powder.

Sastrugi Wind-carved shapes in the snow.

Schussing Running straight down.

Ski brake A device that prevents runaway skis.

Ski mountaineering *See* touring.

Skins Synthetic strips of material that are stuck on to the base of the ski and enable the user to climb uphill.

Slab Snow which breaks into slabs.

Sluff A small loose snow avalanche.

Snow bollard A type of anchor.

Snow hole A shelter dug into the snow.

Snowplough *See* ploughing.

Spring snow Caused by constant freeze-thaw action.

Stemming The action of moving the skis into a wedge shape or plough.

Stufleffer hitch A form of clutch using two different shaped karabiners.

Sunballing Small snowballs set off spontaneously by the heat of the sun on unstable slopes. Not to be confused with those caused by snow dropping from sun-warmed rocks.

Swing to the hill   The second part of a parallel turn.

Telemarking   A form of cross-country skiing which uses the telemark turn.

Touring   Using the skis to travel away from the piste.

Visualising   A mental technique that can enhance performance.

Wedge   *See* snowplough.

White-out   A condition when there is a mist and the snow blends with the sky leaving no discernible horizon.

Windslab   Slab caused by the wind depositing snow.

Bibliography

Avalanches

A Chance in a Million Bob Barton and Blythe Wright (S.M.T.)
Avalanche Symposium Report (Alpine Club)
Avalanches and Snow Safety Colin Fraser (John Murray)
Avalanche Safety for Skiers and Climbers Tony Daffern (Diadem)

General Skiing

Mountain Skiing Vic Bein (The Mountaineers)
Skiing – An Art, A Technique Georges Joubert (Poudre)
Skiing – Developing Your Skill John Shedden (The Crowood
   Press)
Skiing Mechanics John Howe (Poudre)
Skiing Right Horst Abraham (PSIA)
Skilful Skiing John Shedden (EP Publishing Limited)

Mountain Craft

Hill Walking and Scrambling Steve Ashton (The Crowood
   Press)
Medicine for Mountaineers T Wilkenson (The Mountaineers)
Modern Rope Techniques Bill March (Cicerone Press)
Modern Snow and Ice Techniques Bill March (Cicerone Press)
Mountain Craft and Leadership E. Langmuir (Cicerone Press)
Mountain Navigation Peter Cliff (D. E. Thompson)
Mountain Weather David Pedgley (Cicerone Press)
Snow and Ice Climbing John Barry (The Crowood Press)

Index

Also available from The Crowood Press

Cross-Country Skiing *Paddy Field and Tim Walker*
Skiing – Developing Your Skill *John Shedden*
Snow and Ice Climbing *John Barry*
Hill Walking and Scrambling *Steve Ashton*
Rock Climbing *Steve Ashton*
Fitness for Sport *Rex Hazeldine*

Further details of titles available can be obtained from the publishers.